CURIOSITIES OF
TYNESIDE

CURIOSITIES OF
TYNESIDE

ROBERT WOODHOUSE

SUTTON PUBLISHING

First published in 2006 by
Sutton Publishing Limited · Phoenix Mill
Thrupp · Stroud · Gloucestershire · GL5 2BU

British Library Cataloguing in Publication Data
A catalogue record for this book is available from the British Library.

ISBN 0-7509-4444-7

Typeset in 10/11.5pt Janson Text.
Typesetting and origination by
Sutton Publishing Limited.
Printed and bound in England by
J.H. Haynes & Co. Ltd, Sparkford.

To my wife, Sally, who was born and brought up on Tyneside

ABOUT THE AUTHOR

Robert Woodhouse was born in South Yorkshire and educated at Acklam Hall Grammar School, Middlesbrough. An honours degree in history from London University led to a teaching career which spanned some thirty years.

He began writing on local history in the late 1960s and has twenty-four previous books to his credit covering a range of subjects from *River Tees: from source to mouth* to a series of pictorial histories on north-east towns and a trio of 'Strange But True' books on North Yorkshire, County Durham and Northumberland. As well as contributing a weekly walks column to the *Middlesbrough Evening Gazette* (1991–present) he has written six walks books and runs adult education classes covering aspects of north-east history (1981–present).

CONTENTS

Visiting the Curiosities 8

Acknowledgements 9

Introduction 11

Map 12

1. Newcastle 13
2. Gateshead 51
3. North Tyneside 101
4. South Tyneside 113

Index 126

VISITING THE CURIOSITIES

Most of the curiosities featured in this book are accessible without the cost of an admission fee. (An exception is the Gibside estate, near Rowlands Gill, which is owned by the National Trust and normal admission charges and opening times apply.) Some are landmarks, for example the *Angel of the North* and Millennium Bridge, but viewpoints or visitor sites provide close-up perspectives while others are simply features on the external walls of buildings, e.g. the old post office at West Street, Gateshead, and the 'vampire rabbit' at the rear of St Nicholas' Cathedral in Newcastle. Admission to the Victoria Tunnel is by arrangement.

Some featured curiosities are located on private or commercial properties as well as in churchyards, and visitors should show due consideration at these sites. Other settings are in busy urban areas, for example 'Parsons' Polygon' (Newcastle) and the statue of John English (Whickham), and care is needed with regard to traffic.

Most locations are within easy access of the public transport systems and by selective use of a local street plan (obtainable from Tourist Information Centres) they may be grouped together.

ACKNOWLEDGEMENTS

A considerable number of people have assisted with the various aspects of assembling this book and I am greatly indebted to them for a range of advice, support and information. Geoff Underwood, Senior Planner (Conservation) at Gateshead Council, supplied a range of information and lines of research and Anthea Lang, Local History Librarian at Gateshead Library, gave similar support. Local studies departments at North Shields, South Shields, Blaydon and Birtley Libraries also provided valuable assistance.

Phil Thirkell of the Ouseburn Heritage Group gave a considerable amount of help with material relating to the Lower Ouseburn area and Lydia Price, Visitor Services Manager at Gibside (National Trust property), was similarly generous in facilitating research at locations on the Gibside estate. Anna Pepperall, public arts curator at Gateshead Council, provided information about sculptures and artwork in the Gateshead area and Jenny Morrison (Tyne and Wear Archaeology Department) arranged access to a range of materials in the archaeology department's collection.

Reference works from the private collections of several local people were consulted and in this respect I am indebted to Martin Bailey, Lisle Walker and Roy Stephens. Material was also gathered from a host of research papers, old newspapers and local history magazines.

Picture credits are acknowledged to Newcastle City Libraries (photo on page 44), Trevor Ermel (page 99) and Beamish Museum (photos on pages 65, 74 and 90) but the large majority of photographs were taken by the author.

INTRODUCTION

Down the years aspects of Tyneside's varied heritage have been covered in considerable detail with attention paid to industrial development, river trade, church buildings and local personalities and this book represents a collection of landmarks, locations and landscape features that may be termed intriguing, baffling, offbeat or even bizarre.

The area covered by Greater Tyneside extends from sections of coastline on both sides of the Tyne to the rural setting of the Gibside estate on Gateshead's western fringe. Some of the featured items reflect the area's impressive industrial heritage, others are related to colourful local personalities and several are linked with wartime episodes when there was a genuine threat of invasion along England's eastern seaboard.

No compilation of curiosities would be complete without inclusion of the amazing structures that have been at the forefront of Tyneside's cultural regeneration. Their sheer size, scale and overall design seem to epitomise the dynamism and spirit that has been a long-term trademark of Tyneside and its people.

The choice of curiosities is inevitably a personal selection. It is to be hoped that this collection will stimulate discussion and debate. Such ongoing discussion will perhaps ensure that these curiosities continue to generate interest and that this in turn will lead to their long-term preservation.

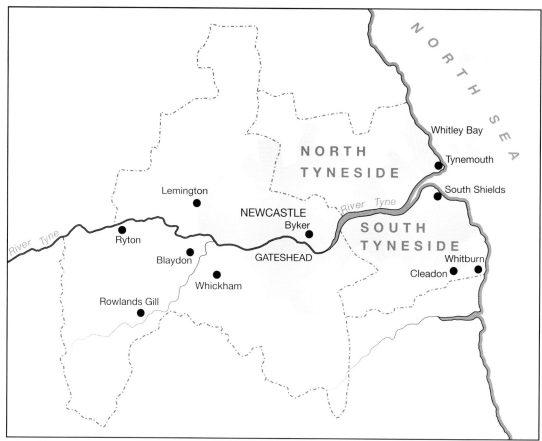

Tyneside.

1

CURIOSITIES
OF NEWCASTLE

A BOLD AND IMAGINATIVE EXERCISE IN MODERN HOUSING

The Byker Wall

Access

The Byker Wall spreads for almost a mile along the south side of Shields Road bypass (on the opposite side of the road from Byker Metro Station) to form a distinctive landmark feature.

No other area of Tyneside has experienced such rapid growth and dramatic change as Byker. Located little more than a mile to the east of Newcastle centre, the township was included within the city boundaries in 1835 during a period of sustained industrial growth. Much of this expansion was linked to the rise of coal, and trades such as shipbuilding, glassmaking and potteries flourished as the

population grew from 3,254 in 1801 to 7,040 in 1851.

Housing spread alongside the Newcastle–North Shields railway (opened 1839) and the Shields turnpike road before the opening of Byker Bridge gave an extra impetus in 1878. A network of terraced streets was built in a grid pattern that sloped in a north–south direction towards the Tyne and east–west towards Ouseburn. Strong social links spread throughout the close-knit community of terraced, cobbled streets, and when problems associated with overcrowding were identified in the 1950s it was seen to be of prime importance that these social ties were maintained during subsequent redevelopment.

Other considerations included the need to shield residents from noise generated by traffic on the planned road systems and to maximise the spectacular views across the river. The architect in charge of redevelopment, Ralph Erskine, and project leader Vernon Gracie consulted local residents as a bold and imaginative scheme was prepared.

The Byker Wall has been termed 'one of the milestones in the development of community architecture' (Nikolaus Pevsner, *The Buildings of England – Northumberland*, Penguin Books, 1992). Spreading for almost a mile, the north face of the Wall was planned to present a barrier against wind and traffic noise with small windows and curious projecting boxes (linked to the ventilation system) scattered along the vertical face. By contrast, the south-facing side included balconies and looked down on courtyards, areas of parkland and pedestrian walkways with distant views across the Tyne.

The height of the Wall ranges from five to nine storeys and the layout was intended to maximise sunlight for as many residents as possible. The futuristic design features included roof coverings of dark blue (in the first phase), bright green (second phase) and blue or green (third phase) but elements of the earlier settlement were included in the form of stone columns and carved stonework from the old Newcastle Town Hall. Stone flags, kerbs and granite chips from old Byker were also installed within the southern precincts.

Phased demolition of old back-to-back properties during the early 1970s saw whole streets of neighbours move into their new homes within the Byker Wall which had easy access to the shopping area on the opposite side of South Shields.

Criticism of the Byker Wall mainly focused on the rear sections rather than the frontages or interiors. The scheme generated widespread interest including a visit by HRH the Duke of Edinburgh on 8 November 1974 (during work on the second phase) and it certainly represented one of the most ambitious and successful architectural projects for decades.

A PRINCE OF RESTING PLACES

The Crown Posada

Access

Crown Posada. A
narrow frontage
on the western
edge of The Side
(at the bottom of
Dean Street) on
the approach to
the Quayside.

Newcastle is renowned for its range of city centre hostelries and while many reflect contemporary trends there are echoes of much earlier days within the princely setting of the Crown Posada.

This outstanding building has operated as an inn for some 230 years and has remained virtually unaltered since the nineteenth century. Its name is derived

from a nineteenth-century owner, a sea captain who had a wife in Spain and a mistress whom he settled at the Crown, as it was then known. He changed the name to Crown Posada because *posada* is the Spanish term for inn or resting place.

The interior retains much of its splendour from those earlier days. Entering from the street outside, the long narrow interior is divided into three sections by mahogany and stained-glass screens. The central area alongside the bar is flanked by a small 'snug' at the front and a lounge at the rear. Much of the atmosphere is derived from a fine mahogany gantry at the back of the bar and a splendid moulded ceiling but the Crown Posada's real treasures are the stained-glass work. In addition to the screens, there is superb glasswork in two external windows. One shows a sad-looking pre-Raphaelite woman filling a glass while the other depicts a cheerful gentleman raising a glass.

BIRTHPLACE OF THE GEORDIE ANTHEM, 'BLAYDON RACES'

Balmbra's

Access

Balmbra's –
known as
Balmbra's Reflex
– is located off
the south-
eastern end of
the Bigg Market
in the Cloth
Market.

The song 'Blaydon Races' is known far and wide as Tyneside's anthem and down the years it has become a rallying call for Geordies wherever they may be based. Composed by George Ridley, he first performed this rousing ballad in 1862 at Newcastle's Wheatsheaf public house and music room. The music hall (which became known as Balmbra's after its owner, John Balmbra) enjoyed great

popularity with local folk during the late nineteenth century but in 1902 it was rebuilt as a public house and billiard hall named the Carlton Hotel.

As the centenary of Geordie Ridley's first performance drew closer a committee of representatives from Newcastle City Council and Blaydon Urban District Council arranged a programme of appropriate events to mark the occasion. A main feature of the occasion was the reopening of Balmbra's, complete with stage and desk for the master of ceremonies. Events on Saturday 9 June 1962 began with a splendid parade featuring more than sixty bands, 160 floats and several hundred people dressed in Victorian costume. In the evening the days of music hall returned with an array of artistes including a troupe of can-can dancers.

This phase of Balmbra's history ended in 1981 but music hall returned to the remarkable venue on 4 April 2000 with a show staged by Leah Bell and her company which included the local comedian, Brendan Healy.

By 2005 the venue had seen another change of name to Balmbra's Reflex but a plaque recalls those earlier glory days when George Ridley first performed the unforgettable song 'Blaydon Races'.

CONTRASTING PLACES OF CARE

Holy Jesus Hospital and the Keelmen's Hospital

Access

Holy Jesus Hospital is at the west end of City Road and adjacent to the Swan House roundabout. It is currently in the care of English Heritage. The Keelmen's Hospital is on City Road overlooking the Quayside and has been adapted as rented accommodation.

A feature of Newcastle's growth as a major urban centre was the presence of five friaries within the city walls, and this may well account for the growth of hospitals and caring institutions around the city.

The Holy Jesus Hospital was built on the site of an Austin friary and opened in 1682 'for the maintenance, sustenation and relief of poor people being Freemen or Freemen's widows'. This fine three-storeyed brick building which included a frontal piazza and ornamental fountain housed a master and thirty-nine inmates. Originally the occupants were given an allowance of £4 per year which was later increased to £6 and then £13.

Another building was added in order to carry out welfare work and its walls had the wording, 'General Soup Kitchen 1880'. The hospital finally closed in 1937 and remained empty and decaying as demolition became a serious consideration. Not only was this impressive structure subsequently saved but it was restored and opened as the John George Joicey Museum with rooms featuring personalities and locations from the last few centuries.

During the late 1960s a new road layout restricted access to the museum and it closed in 1994. It is currently in the care of English Heritage.

Along with shipwrights, watermen and assorted seafarers, keelmen were part of the traditional riverside setting at Newcastle and in 1701 a Keelmen's Hospital was opened on high ground overlooking the Tyne. Supported by the workforce,

this Dutch-style red-brick building provided shelter for old, poor or infirm keelmen and their widows.

Changing trends in river traffic brought the construction of staithes and deepening of the river channel with a resulting decline in the work of keelmen (who transported coal in keel boats to the larger vessels). By 1782 the Society of Keelmen had been abolished but in recent years this landmark building with its distinctive central tower has been adapted as student accommodation.

BRIDGES OF DISTINCTION

The Ouseburn

Access

The Ouseburn area is west of Byker and north of the A186 Walker Road.

In recent years projects along the banks of the Tyne at Gateshead and Newcastle have attracted widespread interest and publicity, making it easy to overlook the importance and significance of areas beside the Ouseburn on the western side of Newcastle city centre.

The fording point close to the Ouseburn Farm has probably been in use since the Roman period and the eight bridges in the locality all hold a certain amount of interest. Crawford's Bridge is the oldest bridge in the city still in use and probably dates from the mid-eighteenth century at a time when Thomas Crawford owned several properties in the vicinity including Crawford's Row.

When the Newcastle and North Shields Railway was constructed between 1837 and 1839 the engineers for the project were John and Benjamin Green and their section of line included two viaducts at Ouseburn and further east at Willington Gut. They are unusual because laminated timber arch construction was applied in making use of the Wiebeking system.

The original Ouseburn Viaduct had five spans and measured 918ft in length with building work carried out by J. Welch & Company. During 1869 the timber

arches were replaced with ironwork supplied by the Weardale Iron & Steel Company and it was widened to carry four tracks in 1885.

These two viaducts are believed to be the earliest laminated timber arch railway bridges in Britain. Plans were made for a similar structure across the Tyne but this ambitious scheme did not materialise. However, laminated arches were

favoured by many other bridge builders after the success of the Green brothers' design work at Ouseburn and Willington.

The nearby road viaduct represents another impressive example of civil engineering and the Byker viaduct, which carries the Tyne & Wear Metro system across the valley, includes aspects of considerable significance to bridge builders.

A DUMPING GROUND, RECREATION AREA AND A DISAPPEARING GRAVEYARD

Ballast Hills

Access

The Ballast Hills area was located in the Lower Ouseburn area around the former Ouseburn school (now the Quayside Business Development Centre).

Until the advent of steam ships (when water was used to provide stability) vessels arriving in the Tyne carried a whole range of commodities as ballast. All sailing ships carried some form of ballast such as scrap metal, building rubble, sand, flints and broken glass which was carried on their heads from the ships by women and dumped on riverside slopes to the east of Newcastle.

Newcastle Corporation gained large amounts of income by leasing land for tipping and as trade increased on the Tyne so the ballast hills became a distinctive feature of the landscape. Slippage caused problems along the river's edge but these extraordinary man-made contours soon became popular venues for sporting events as well as serving more practical purposes such as drying areas for clothes. These practices became so entrenched that when plans were announced for construction of a limekiln, in 1633, there was an outbreak of rioting.

The Ballast Hills graveyard at Ouseburn saw its first burials possibly as early as the plague year of 1609, and its continued use through the eighteenth century saw it become the most important Nonconformist burial ground in the Newcastle area. Housing was built on all sides and during 1785 funds were raised to build a boundary wall and gravedigger's house. Most burials were local folk from an industrial background but a number of Nonconformist ministers were also laid to

rest here. These include the Revd John Cawley (1723–92) who was described by John Wesley as one of the best preachers in England.

The graveyard was unused from 1853 when a cholera epidemic forced closure of all burial grounds. In 1930 the burial area was landscaped by the corporation as a children's play area and surviving gravestones were laid flat to form pathways. Other stones, including those of several Nonconformist ministers, were placed in an upright position close to the red-brick school buildings.

NEWCASTLE'S OLDEST CHAPEL

St Mary's Chapel and Well, Jesmond

Until the mid-nineteenth century Jesmond was little more than a village located between the Ouseburn and the city of Newcastle. Since then it has become a popular residential setting with all the features of a modern suburb – but among an oasis of woodland, in the heart of Jesmond, stand the remains of Newcastle's oldest church or chapel.

St Mary's Chapel was probably built by the Grenville family during the early twelfth century but the first documentary reference appears in an Assize Roll of 1272. It gives details of an episode when five priests helped a prisoner escape from jail in Newcastle and then guided him to St Mary's Chapel before escorting him to Tynemouth.

During the following centuries this tiny place of worship had many owners ranging from monarchs (such as Edward III in 1364) to the mayor and citizens of Newcastle (in 1594) at a time when it included a nearby hospice. Lord Armstrong made use of the monastic buildings as a barn and stable before handing it over to the city authorities.

Access

St Mary's Chapel and Well are on open grassland reached from Jesmond Dene Road and The Grove.

Along with the nearby well, the site has been a place of pilgrimage for many centuries. 'Divers miracles' were said to have come about among sick people visiting the chapel and it has been suggested that the route followed by pilgrims led to the naming of Pilgrim Street in Newcastle.

St Mary's Well lies about 200 yards to the west of the chapel and included a stone head with the Latin inscription, '*Ave Maria Gratia Plena*' (Hail Mary Full of Grace). Only the word '*Gratia*' survives on the stonework.

During cold weather warm water bubbling from the spring produced a cloud of vapour and the well's reputation for healing powers has continued until recent times with people continuing to fill bottles with the water. The site was transferred to the corporation in 1932 and during 1982 archaeological excavations revealed that the existing stonework only dates from the seventeenth century. It is believed that one of the two other springs in this secluded location may be the source of the tales of miraculous cures from bubbling waters.

FASHIONABLE RESIDENCE IN AN INDUSTRIAL SETTING

Clavering House, Forth Street

Construction of bridging points across the Tyne during the nineteenth and twentieth centuries sliced through whole sectors of Newcastle's fashionable areas and it seems amazing that Clavering House survived intact. Situated close to the east end of Forth Street, this splendid Grade II listed property is dwarfed by railway arches but retains its late eighteenth-century dignity. Built for Sir Thomas Clavering in the mid-1780s, it stands close to Hanover Square which was begun in 1720 with a name taken from the first Hanoverian king, George I.

From 1830 to 1850 Clavering House was the home of Sir Robert Shafto Hawks and his family and in recent years the interior of the property has been adapted as office accommodation.

Access

Clavering House stands close to the east end of Forth Street near the arches of the High Level Bridge.

A ROMANTIC ELOPEMENT

Bessie Surtees' House, Sandhill

Access

Bessie Surtees'
House dominates
the roadside at
the western side
of the Quayside
at Sandhill.

Sectors of downtown Newcastle have seen successive phases of redevelopment but some locations retain fine examples of earlier architectural styles. The Sandhill area is situated close to the Tyne Bridge and includes some of the city's finest frontages. Probably the best known of these is Bessie Surtees' House which dates from the seventeenth century when it was owned by a wealthy banker, Aubone Surtees. The eldest of his eight children was an attractive daughter, Elizabeth, who was courted by John Scott, the son of a coal merchant based in nearby Love Lane. Bessie's father strongly objected to the burgeoning romance and the courting couple were forced to meet in secret.

Matters came to a head when Aubone Surtees arranged for Bessie to marry 63-year-old Sir Walter Blackett. John Scott persuaded Bessie to elope with him to Scotland where they married under Scottish law at Blackshields. The dramatic departure by ladder from the family home on 18 November 1772 is illustrated in a painting by Wilson Hepple.

The young couple were later reunited with their parents and married according to English law. John Scott took up a career in law and was called to the bar in 1776. The next few years saw him established as a highly successful barrister and in 1783 he gained a parliamentary seat. During 1788 he was appointed Solicitor-General and awarded a knighthood.

Scott's successful parliamentary career saw him hold the posts of Attorney General, Lord Chief Justice of Common Pleas, Baron Eldon, Lord High Chancellor and Earl of Eldon. (His links with Newcastle are celebrated in the City's Eldon Square.)

The splendid five-storeyed Bessie Surtees' House represents a fine example of Jacobean domestic architecture. It is now in the care of English Heritage.

LAST SURVIVOR OF NEWCASTLE'S RELIGIOUS HOUSES

Blackfriars

Access

Blackfriars is bounded by The Gave, Stowell Street and Charlotte Square. It incorporates a range of workshops and business units.

An unusual feature of medieval Newcastle was the number of monastic houses within the city walls. Blackfriars represents the last reminder of five friaries and rates as one of the city's oldest surviving buildings. The order of Dominican or Black Friars were based in Newcastle upon Tyne from 1239 and it is believed that the city's first Lord Mayor, Sir Peter Scott, assisted with the building costs. The site was close to the line later taken by the city walls at the western edge of the city and during the fourteenth century a number of English monarchs visited Blackfriars with donations of corn, cloth, wine and money for the friars. During 1334 Edward Balliol arrived to pay homage for the Kingdom of Scotland to King Edward III.

In 1537 Richard Marshall, Prior of the Dominicans and a strong supporter of the Papacy, fled the country in the face of closure by Henry VIII's commissioners. Some six years later Blackfriars was sold to the mayor and burgess of Newcastle for £53 7s 6d and from 1552 trade guilds occupied the premises which had been divided into nine separate units.

By the 1960s the buildings had deteriorated badly and in 1972 only the Tailors' and Smiths' Halls were fit for occupation. During 1973 a company of architects from Skipton (Wales, Wales & Rawson) completed survey work and by 1977 most of the west range had been restored. Over the next three years the south and east ranges were refurbished at a total overall cost of £600,000, and the whole project was given royal approval in April 1980 when Queen Elizabeth the Queen Mother unveiled a plaque as part of Newcastle's 900th anniversary celebrations.

Blackfriars now houses a range of craft workshops and business units.

A CHURCH WITH AN UNUSUAL OVAL-SHAPED DESIGN

All Saints Church

Access

All Saints Church covers a plot overlooking the Quayside and the tower is a prominent landmark. It is currently used as a place of worship by the Anglican Old Catholic Church of St Willibrord.

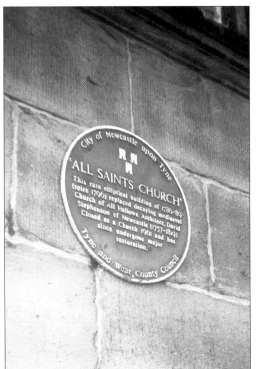

The tower of All Saints Church became a landmark on Newcastle's skyline when it was completed in the early 1790s to designs by David Stephenson, but it is the unusual ground plan that gives it an even greater measure of interest. Replacing the medieval church of All Hallows, the overall layout of All Saints represents one of few oval-shaped churches in Britain and features such as a detached portico with four Greek Doric columns and sections of balustrading undoubtedly influenced Sir John Betjeman's description of this Quayside church as 'one of the finest English Georgian churches'. Following deconsecration in 1961, it was adapted for use as office accommodation, but in recent years it has been reconsecrated as the Anglican Old Catholic Church of St Willibrord.

STILL MAKING HEADLINE NEWS

Tyneside Cinema

Access

Tyneside Cinema
is prominent on
the north side of
Pilgrim Street.

The Tyneside Cinema in Pilgrim Street, Newcastle, has a place in the history of the modern film industry. Built in 1937 as the News Theatre, it currently shows films from all over the world and represents the last surviving purpose-built newsreel cinema in the country that is still showing films.

During the early days of 2006 it was announced that £3 million funding had been received from the Heritage Lottery Fund. A further £500,000 sum from the

Northern Rock Foundation formed the basis of finances that would allow restoration work aimed at giving an appreciation of contemporary lifestyles in the 1930s and '40s. Cinema historians point to the importance of this type of cinema during the late 1930s when newsreels, topical interest films and cartoons were shown. In the years before television they served an important function in spreading information and were opened in city centres and main line railway stations. An interesting aspect of the Tyneside Cinema is the ornate second-floor cinema café.

LAIR OF THE MANIC RABBIT

Amen Corner

There are any number of quiet settings within easy reach of Newcastle's bustling city centre but few hold the sort of surprise that lurks beyond the east end of St Nicholas's churchyard.

   A row of impressive brick-built properties lines the roadway leading to Amen Corner with decorative architectural features on the solicitor's office (of 1901) catching the eye. Yet among all the traditional design work, the lower section of a large circular window is dominated by the dark grey-painted sculpture of a large rabbit. Complete with oversized canine teeth and with a fearsome expression on its face, this bewildering beast has become known as the 'Vampire Rabbit'.

Access

The so-called 'manic rabbit' peers down on the east end of St Nicholas's Cathedral from the rear of premises on Dean Street close to Amen Corner.

STREET SCULPTURE WITH A SCIENTIFIC BENT

Parsons' Polygon, Blackett Street

Access

Parsons' Polygon is located on the north side of the roadway in Blackett Street close to the junction with Blackett Place.

In recent years sculptures have become a feature of many town and city centres. Sometimes artistic appeal is combined with a practical function, and this is certainly the case with the Parsons' Polygon at the junction of Newcastle's Blackett Street and Blackett Place.

Described by its sculptor, David Hamilton, as 'a mixture of restraints and opportunities', this curious roadside structure stands 10ft in height. It was commissioned by the Tyne & Wear Passenger Transport Executive (Nexus) as part of the Art on Metro Scheme and represents the only piece of Metro artwork located outside a station. In fact this mini-tower serves as a ventilation shaft for the metro station below and panels on its sides celebrate the achievements of an inventor from the early twentieth century.

Sir Charles Parsons (1854–1931) masterminded construction of the turbine-powered *Turbinia* that achieved a speed of more than 30 knots at the Naval Review held at Spithead in June 1897 to celebrate Queen Victoria's Diamond Jubilee. Designs on the light red coloured sides of the Polygon have been made to represent interpretations of Parsons' engineering drawings.

A PENNY BAZAAR THAT IS STILL GOING STRONG

The Grainger Market

The Grainger Market was an important element of Thomas Grainger's redevelopment of Newcastle city centre. Covering some 2 acres of ground, it was regarded by some contemporary observers as the finest shopping area of its kind in Europe. Fourteen entrances gave access to this impressive covered market where four long alleys ran from north to south and four short passages led at right angles from these. An opening banquet was arranged for 2,000 guests and ladies were 'permitted to watch from the balcony'.

Within the market a Marks & Spencer Penny Bazaar was opened in 1895, the second in the country after the original one had begun trading in Kirkgate, Leeds. The Grainger Market had opened in 1835 and there were echoes of that original grand ceremony on the 150th anniversary in 1985 when market traders dressed in period costumes. Meanwhile the Marks & Spencer Bazaar continues to trade into the twenty-first century from the same premises and with original fittings from the original opening in 1895.

Access

The Penny Bazaar is at the north-eastern sector of the Grainger Market which is south of the Eldon Square Shopping Centre.

Chinese Charms on Tyneside

The Chinese Arch, Stowell Street

Access

The Chinese Arch spans the roadway at the north-eastern edge of Chinatown where St Andrew's Street meets Gallowgate.

During 2002 plans were prepared for a six-year scheme for the regeneration of the Grainger Town area of Newcastle. An element of the project was the construction of a Chinese arch at the northern end of Stowell Street with the twin purpose of boosting business and providing a visitor attraction. Similar gateways were already in place within the Chinatown areas of other places such as Manchester, and the colourful elements of this ornamental archway certainly provide a talking point. Its exotic eastern charms are highlighted further by the towering steelwork of the nearby St James' Park Stadium, home of Newcastle United FC.

A TOUCH OF THE ORIENT ON DEEPEST TYNESIDE

Ouseburn School

In many respects the red brickwork of Ouseburn School is very similar to many other late Victorian school buildings. Completed in 1893 to designs by architect Frank Wise Rich, the layout was known as the 'Central Hall' system, with rooms for training in cookery, laundry work, drawing and manual tasks around the middle area – but it is the ornate top sections of the corner towers that attract attention.

Looking like fanciful pagodas, they contrast markedly with the simple outlines of the lower brickwork and although local gossip suggested that they were meant to reflect the work for the Japanese Navy at nearby shipyards the truth is rather less romantic. They represent an important feature of the school's plenum system of heating and ventilation. Air in rooms throughout the building was maintained during the year at a constant temperature by a system of radiators and pipes which introduced fresh warm air and ventilated each area through tubes that ran through shafts into the elaborate pagoda-style towers.

The premises now house the Quayside Business Development Centre.

Access

The former Ouseburn School is prominent on the north side of the A186 on the west side of Byker.

A UNIQUE URBAN SETTING

Newcastle Town Moor

Access

The Town Moor lies on the west side of the Great North Road on the north side of Newcastle city centre.

References to Newcastle's Town Moor date back more than 700 years and the preservation of such an area of open ground so close to the city is said to be unique in Britain.

During the reign of King John, in 1213, this sizeable area of land was defined as common ground, and during 1357 Edward III's officials restated the rights in common law. The Freemen of Newcastle are thought to have enjoyed grazing rights on the moor for many centuries before they were reaffirmed in the Town Moor Act of 1774. These were confirmed by a further round of legislation in 1988.

The Royal Commission on Historical Monuments completed a detailed archaeological survey of the Town Moor in 1996. Their research identified a whole range of human activity including a prehistoric settlement, medieval and later ploughing patterns, traces of eighteenth- and nineteenth-century racecourses, remnants of the 1929 North East Coast Exhibition, Second World War defences and features from an Italian prisoner-of-war camp.

Various areas of the Town Moor extend over a total of around 1,000 acres, and management remains with the City Council which owns the land and Freemen of the City, who hold grazing rights.

In 1721 the annual Northumberland race meeting was moved from Killingworth to the Town Moor and it continued there until 1882 when horse racing was relocated to Gosforth Park. During race week a temperance festival was staged with the emphasis on children's games, military competitions and travelling fairs. The festival was held on an annual basis until 1912 and after returning to the Town Moor in 1924 the festivities known locally as the 'hoppings' continued until the outbreak of the Second World War. In 1947 fairground attractions returned to this fascinating location and with the event increasing in popularity it is widely regarded as the largest non-permanent fair in the world.

A STRIKING REMINDER OF AN EARLY INDUSTRY

Lemington Glass Cone

Access

Lemington glass
cone is a
landmark on the
west side of the
A1 (Western
Bypass) close to
the A6085.

The Lemington glass cone is a striking reminder of an industry that developed during the early seventeenth century after glassmakers arrived on Tyneside from Lorraine. Glassmaking soon began on the south side of the Tyne at South Shields where workers specialised in plate-glassmaking and by 1827 eight large-scale glassworks had been opened. Production went from strength to strength and during the period 1827–45 more plate glass was made at South Shields than at any other location in the British Isles.

One of the most prosperous operations in the Newcastle area was at Lemington to the west of the city where an exceptionally large cone was constructed in 1787. A structure of this type enabled glass blowing to take place in well-ventilated but not draughty surroundings.

Other cones on the site have been removed but the single glasshouse was preserved by Messrs Glass Tube & Components Ltd. Measuring over 100ft in height, it is one of only five that remain in the country and as well as representing a local landmark it provides a fitting reminder of one of Tyneside's less well-known industries.

'THE BLINKING EYE'

The Millennium Bridge

The Millennium Bridge spans the Tyne between Baltic Square on the Gateshead side and Newcastle's Quayside.

There have been bridges across the lower Tyne since the Emperor Hadrian's engineers constructed the first crossing point in about AD 120 but there has never before been anything like the magnificent Millennium Bridge.

Officially opened on 17 September 2001, some five years after the concept was formulated, it cost £22 million and represents the world's first rotating bridge. With design work by Wilkinson Eyre, Architects, and engineering operations completed by Gifford & Partners, the superstructure weighs more than 835 tons and stands on a massive base composed of 18,000 tons of concrete.

The span measures 413ft and pivots to a fully open position in four minutes with power supplied from eight motors. A pedestrian walkway of solid steel runs side by side with a cycle track made from perforated aluminium. Another design feature ensures that litter is gathered in containers every time the bridge is tilted.

The Millennium Bridge represents the seventh river crossing in the sector covered by Gateshead and central Newcastle but it is certainly very different from any that have gone before.

UNDER THE TYNE

Tyneside's Other Tunnels

During recent years the Tyne's vehicular tunnel has attracted regular rounds of publicity but other tunnels on Tyneside are less well known. In 1946 plans were drawn up for three tunnels under the Tyne but an estimated cost of £3,600,000 meant that work was restricted to pedestrian and cyclist tunnels.

Construction work began in June 1947 and engineers were soon faced with a range of sub-terranean conditions as well as problems posed by the workings of the old Jarrow and Howdon Collieries. The completed tunnels were opened by Alfred Barnes MP (Minister of Transport) on 24 July 1951 and the Waygood Otis escalators at either end of the tunnel had the largest single lift in Britain (with a vertical rise of 85ft). Work on the vehicular tunnel took almost exactly six years (from October 1961 to

Access

The vehicular tunnel carries traffic on the A19 from the south bank at Jarrow to Howdon on the north side.

Access

Pedestrian and
cyclist tunnels
are slightly
upstream from
the vehicular
tunnel and run
from Jarrow to
Willington Quay.

October 1967) and completed the trio of underground routes between
Jarrow and the north bank of the Tyne.

During the 1830s engineers were faced with the problem of transporting coal from the Spital Tongues Colliery on the north-west side of
Newcastle to coal staithes on the Tyne. Overland routes around the town
centre were not viable and on 27 June 1839 work began on an
underground wagonway. The completed project was formally opened on
7 April 1842 and was named Victoria Tunnel in honour of the reigning
monarch.

Engineers on this nineteenth-century project may well have used
methods employed in an earlier 'subterraneous wagon' that was completed

in the late eighteenth century to move
coal some 3 miles from Kenton Colliery to
the banks of the Tyne at Scotswood.

The completed Victoria Tunnel was
over 2 miles in length and descended 222ft
on the single-track route from colliery to
river bank with a greatest depth of 85ft
below the surface. Operations soon
brought a reduction in the cost of transporting coal but for about eighty years,
from 1860, this underground wagonway
remained unused.

During the Second World War sections
of the tunnel were adapted for use as air
raid shelters with basic accommodation
for 9,000 people at a cost of £37,000. The
central section of the tunnel runs below
central Newcastle at a depth of about 40ft
and blast walls were constructed during
the war.

In recent years the tunnel has remained
unused apart from staging scientific
experiments for students from Newcastle

Access

The Victoria
Tunnel ran from
Spital Tongues
Colliery on the
north-west side
of Newcastle to
the banks of the
Tyne at
Ouseburn
(sections of the
tunnel are closed
but arrangements
are made to visit
the remaining
sections from
time to time).

University and although sections have been closed off it represents an important industrial structure from Tyneside's coal-mining heyday.

The section of tunnel through the Lower Ouseburn Valley is maintained by Ouseburn Heritage Group and Newcastle City Council. Visits are arranged by the Ouseburn Heritage Trust.

were happy to accept a tunnel. Consequently work was begun on what was to become the "Victoria Tunnel" in June 1839 and completed in January 1842. The tunnel was formally opened, in the presence of the Mayor of Newcastle, on 7th April 1842.

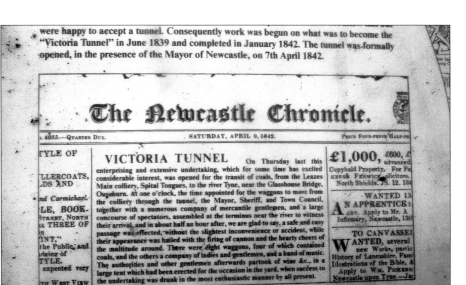

The Newcastle Chronicle.

4055.—QUARTER DUE.   SATURDAY, APRIL 9, 1842.   PRICE FOUR-PENCE HALF-PE

VICTORIA TUNNEL On Thursday last this enterprising and extensive undertaking, which for some time has excited considerable interest, was opened for the transit of coals, from the Leazes Main colliery, Spital Tongues, to the river Tyne, near the Glasshouse Bridge, Ouseburn. At one o'clock, the time appointed for the waggons to move from the colliery through the tunnel, the Mayor, Sheriff, and Town Council, together with a numerous company of mercantile gentlemen, and a large concourse of spectators, assembled at the terminus near the river to witness their arrival, and in about half an hour after, we are glad to say, a safe and easy passage was effected, without the slightest inconvenience or accident, while their appearance was hailed with the firing of cannon and the hearty cheers of the multitude around. There were eight waggons, four of which contained coals, and the others a company of ladies and gentlemen, and a band of music. The authorities and other gentlemen afterwards partook of wine &c., in a large tent which had been erected for the occasion in the yard, when success to the undertaking was drunk in the most enthusiastic manner by all present.

Contemporary newspaper reporting the opening of the tunnel.

THE TUNNEL AT WORK

The tunnel proved to be an efficient and less expensive way of transporting coal. It was reported that the owners had cut their transport costs to an eighth of their previous level. However the colliery itself was not a success. Within ten years it was not regularly working and by 1857 it was being offered for sale and by 1860 was closed entirely. The tunnel had been used for less than eighteen years.

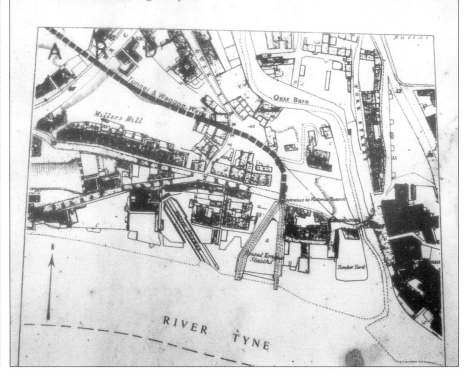

2

CURIOSITIES
OF GATESHEAD

AN AMAZING COLLECTION OF ARTWORKS

Public Arts Programme, Gateshead

Access

Artworks feature at locations throughout the area from elevated hilltop positions to the Riverside Sculpture Park and town centre sites. *Sports Day* dominates the pedestrian walkway on West Street. *The Family* cover open grassland outside the office of Births, Marriages and Deaths at Gateshead Civic Centre. *Threshold* forms an archway at the southern end of the High Street.

Since the early 1980s Gateshead Council has developed a Public Arts Programme which has gained widespread recognition and a string of awards. An impressive range of artworks have been installed at locations throughout the area and several such as *The Angel of the North* and *Windy Nook* have become landmarks in their

own right. Several sculptures are sited in the Riverside Sculpture Park and others have been positioned on Gateshead's main streets.

Sports Day in West Street was completed on site by Mike Winstone, Gateshead's sculptor in residence during 1985–6. Standing more than 12ft in height, it is made of reinforced painted concrete and draws on Gateshead's sporting reputation for inspiration. Rather than reflecting taut muscles and a dramatic pose, the figure is portrayed in the amusing setting of a sack race which communicates the exuberance of a school sports day.

There are similar massive dimensions to Gordon Young's set of three carvings outside Gateshead Civic Centre. Sited near the Office of Births, Marriages and Deaths the sets of linked figures symbolise life's main stages of infancy, maturity and old age. *The Family* was fashioned from Cumbrian limestone and the process of chipping, drilling and polishing lasted three years before the figures were completed in 1991.

Other artworks feature in diverse locations ranging from subways in Hepper Street (the 'Blue Subway') and Barns Close (the 'Orpheus Subway') to Beacons which stand almost 20ft high around the Gateshead Quays, but the most innovative must be *Threshold*. It is a unique, interactive sound sculpture which

takes the shape of a large-scale stainless steel doorway across the pedestrian route at the southern end of the High Street.

As people pass under the arch a sensor is activated and sounds, songs and stories with local connections are played. These feature schoolchildren, a male voice choir and animals from Bill Quay Farm. *Threshold* is illuminated at night by LED lights and received a prestigious Civic Trust Award in 2004.

INCREDIBLE DESIGN FEATURES OF THE SAGE, GATESHEAD

The Sage, Gateshead

Few modern buildings can include as many spectacularly innovative features as the Sage at Gateshead. Opened on 17 December 2004 at a cost of £70 million, it forms the centrepiece of Gateshead Quays which includes the Millennium Bridge and Baltic Centre for Contemporary Art.

Primarily it was a purpose-built base for all kinds of music but the design work of Lord Norman Foster reflects the earlier innovative and imaginative projects along Gateshead's river frontage. A dramatic glazed concourse spreads around the front and sides to link three music halls, a music education centre and entertainment rooms. Construction work also maximised acoustic quality by employing the specialist company, Arup Acoustics, which incorporated sound-

Access

The Sage dominates the central area of Gateshead Quays close to the Millennium Bridge and the Baltic Centre for Contemporary Art.

absorbing curtains and adjustable ceiling panels in order to provide ideal conditions for performances ranging from the spoken word to full orchestral settings and amplified music.

Other sectors of this amazing structure include a café, bars and brasserie as well as a music information centre named Explore Music, while spectacular views of the River Tyne add to the stunning appeal of this outstanding building.

Spreading like a series of huge glazed shells, the Sage's exterior provokes endless discussion and debate but it is the range of striking internal features that ensure this remarkable venue's position as an international arts facility.

FROM FLOUR MILLS TO CENTRE FOR CONTEMPORARY ART

The Baltic Flour Mills

In recent years the banks of the Tyne at Gateshead and Newcastle have witnessed dramatic changes with earlier industrial settings swept away to accommodate an amazing range of futuristic structures. Yet one building survived and after an incredible transformation it has taken on an entirely new role.

Construction of the Baltic Flour Mills began in the 1930s and after a delay during the war years, 1939–45, work restarted in 1948. After opening in 1950 the mills became a dual-purpose factory for the production of flour and animal feed but business slumped after a serious fire in 1976 and after demolition and clearance work during 1982 only one of the mill buildings remained.

In 1994 a competition was held to choose a design which would convert the silo warehouse into an international centre for contemporary art and four years later internal concrete grain silos were removed to leave external brick walls held in place by a steel brace. A so-called 'kittiwake tower' was constructed on the site to relocate a colony of seabirds from their nesting positions within the derelict building.

With access to the main structure from the low-slung Riverside Building, the Baltic incorporates five different galleries, rooftop restaurant, viewing box and external viewing terrace.

This new structure opened to the public on 13 July 2002 and ranks as one of the largest contemporary arts venues of its type in Europe, offering a wide range of educational activities and events for people of all ages and abilities.

Access

The Baltic stands at the eastern end of Gateshead Quays with vehicular access by Mill Road and pedestrian access from the riverside.

ANCIENT HILL FORT OR MODERN WORK OF ART?

Windy Nook

Access

Windy Nook
spreads around
the summit of an
elevated mound
at the junction of
Sundew Road
and Whitehill
Drive on
Gateshead's
south-eastern
fringe. A car park
is at the bottom
of the southern
slope.

Gateshead's series of modern sculptures spreads throughout the township and Richard Cole's puzzling collection of stone terraces dominates high ground on the south-eastern sector. Completed in 1986, *Windy Nook* stands 520ft high and covers 60,000sq ft to represent one of Europe's largest environmental sculptures.

This huge composition converted an unsightly colliery slag heap into a

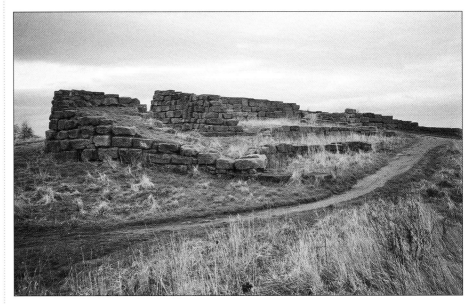

formidable piece of land art. The terraced design consists of concentric semi-circular stone walls and turfed earthworks running down the hillside and including 2,500 tons of granite recycled from pillars supporting the old Scotswood Bridge.

Richard Cole attempted to work on a scale appropriate to the elevated hill site and create an organic structure in keeping with the immediate environment. Since its completion, this massive stone feature has blended naturally into its surroundings with the result that local residents and visitors speculate about its origins as an ancient hill fort rather than a recent work of art.

MEMORIES OF A LOCAL BRICKWORKS

Blythe's Pillar

Access

Blythe's pillar stands in the churchyard of St Joseph's Catholic Church on Birtley Lane on the western side of the A1 south of Gateshead.

Thomas Blythe opened a brickworks at Birtley station in 1858 and the company's red vans helped to spread the reputation of 'Blythe's Best Birtley Bricks'. In about 1910 Jack Blythe purchased a number of stones from part of the old steeple of Chester-le-Street Parish Church and rebuilt them as a 12ft high pillar in the churchyard of St Joseph's Roman Catholic Church on Birtley Lane. Some three years later he added a crucifix to the stone pillar.

Blythe's motto was 'The bricks that will endure as long as bricks are used' but the company – which at one time had a workforce of about thirty – stopped production in 1978.

POIGNANT TRIBUTE TO A LOCAL CHAMPION

James Renforth

The area's strong links with river-based sports are illustrated by a dramatic monument that stands outside Gateshead Shipley Art Gallery on Prince Consort Road. Topped by a block which has a reclining figure cradling another man in his arms above ocean waves, it is a memorial to a fine oarsman. Beneath this topmost section are the poignant words, 'In the midst of life we are in death', and the central portion of this massive memorial reads 'James Renforth champion sculler of the world who died August 1871 aged 29 while rowing in an international boat race between English and American crews on the Kennebecassis near St John's Nova Scotia'.

Access

The monument stands by the roadside south of the city centre on Prince Consort Road.

MONUMENTS TO A LOCAL SPORTING HERO . . . AND HIS MOTHER

Henry Clasper

Access

The Clasper memorials are located in St Mary's churchyard on the north side of the B6317 close to the centre of Whickham.

Down the years Tyneside has produced any number of sporting heroes but even with a splendid statue marking his grave in Whickham churchyard the achievements of the world champion rower, Henry Clasper, remain largely unknown.

Born on the banks of the Tyne at Derwenthaugh, he and his son built boats at Brown's boathouse in Durham. Henry Clasper is said to have rowed on almost every river in the country and took the national title from Thames boatmen for the first time before triumphing in the world championships. He died in July 1870 and a massive crowd of people numbering 130,000 is said to have lined the banks of the Tyne as his body was carried by barge to St Mary's churchyard at Whickham, where a magnificent monument marks his final resting place. It is composed of a sandstone statue and is set on a square base with inscribed panels while a tall octagonal canopy adds a further stately dimension.

Close at hand stands the tomb of Jane Clasper, mother of Henry. She died in 1849 and this highly unusual memorial was erected by her sons. It takes the form of a thin, pointed column which is meant to represent an up-ended racing skiff.

A BELGIAN COLONY
IN THE CENTRE OF BIRTLEY

'Elisabethville'

Wartime contingencies produced many unusual situations but few are more remarkable than events linked with the establishment of a Belgian 'colony' at Birtley during the First World War.

By the early weeks of 1915 there was a serious shortage of artillery shells and the British government reached agreement with private firms about building and operating National Projectile Factories. The north-east area had a number of advantages in terms of coal deposits, chemical works and the iron and steel

Access

Lamesley Road Garage is one of few buildings that remain from 'Elisabethville' in the southern sector of Birtley.

industry so in July 1915 an agreement was reached between the government and Armstrong-Whitworth to build two factories at Birtley. One would manufacture shells and the other cartridge cases, and production began during the summer of 1916.

The workforce was to consist of Belgians and, with limited accommodation available in local homes, the decision was taken to build a self-contained village which became known as the 'huts'. Covering some 95 acres and with living space for about 5,000 Belgian refugees, the new settlement had its own police force (or gendarmerie), small prison, hospital, communal restaurant, school, post office and other facilities. The whole area was surrounded by a tall iron railing with gates at intervals and it was given the name 'Elisabethville' in honour of the Belgian queen at the time.

The camp was run on strict military lines and after months of tension rioting broke out on 21 December 1916. A workman was imprisoned for wearing civilian clothes and other workmen then attacked the police station. When a gendarme opened fire a small boy was wounded and as tension grew the rioters threatened to burn down the village camp. It took the intervention of a British official and release of the prisoner to calm the situation.

A committee of inquiry reported in favour of the workmen and concessions were made in order to improve conditions. Families were allowed to join the menfolk and British policemen replaced the Belgian gendarmes but Elisabethville remained closed to local Birtley residents until the whole community celebrated the declaration of armistice on 11 November 1918.

Less than a month later, on 7 December 1918, three passenger trains left Birtley on the way to Hull with returning Belgian families. A few Belgians stayed behind and integrated into the local community while many of the huts were used to house British ex-servicemen who were retraining in practical skills such as tailoring and upholstery.

During the interwar years the Rural District Council used the huts to accommodate the growing population of Birtley, but by 1938 many people had been moved to the newly built Barley Mow estate. This curious 'colony' known locally as 'the huts' was later replaced by a council estate named Elisabethville. Apart from the name, there are few traces of the wartime settlement but the cemetery, a short section of iron railings and two huts (which are now used as a garage) represent a fascinating legacy from events on the home front some ninety years ago.

INTRIGUING BUILDINGS IN CENTRAL GATESHEAD

Central Public House and the Old Post Office Building

Gateshead town centre has a whole range of contrasting buildings, sculptures and architectural features. Successive phases of redevelopment have replaced many of the town's earlier landmarks with modern and innovative architectural designs but a couple of intriguing structures have survived.

Access

The Central public house faces Half Moon Lane near the bottle bank close to the Tyne Bridge.

Access

The old post
office building
stands on West
Street to the
north of the
Central Square
and shopping
area.

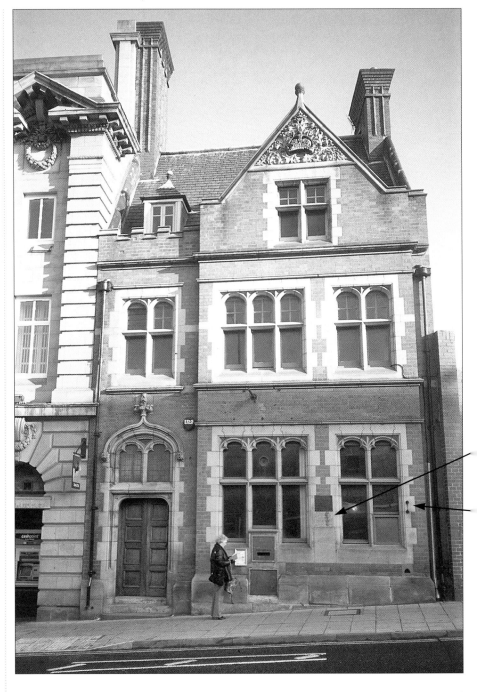

The aptly named Central public house building dominates the strip of ground fronting Half Moon Lane where its distinctive shape and contrasting architectural features create a most unusual landmark. Affectionately nicknamed 'the coffin', it was built by John Potts, a former mayor of Gateshead, and remains one of the town's oldest public houses.

The old post office building on West Street opened on 1 July 1897 and has many traditional late nineteenth-century attributes but it is a couple of small features close to the ground floor windows that hold particular interest. Brickwork in the lower level of the wall has a vertical metal handle above a concave groove in a sandstone panel. These simple devices allowed a policeman on patrol in central Gateshead to lift himself above the window ledge and check that all was well inside the rooms within the building.

Plaques on the outside wall state that Thomas Bewick, the artist and engraver, lived in a building on the site up to his death in 1828. The post office included for the first time in Gateshead a telegraph delivery office and was very unusual for those days as it employed four female clerks.

It closed in 2004 and has since been used by a health organisation.

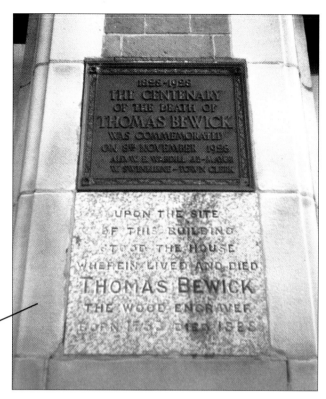

EVER-CHANGING PLACE OF WORSHIP, CARE AND SUPPORT

Trinity Community Centre

Access

Trinity Community Centre is prominent on the east side of Gateshead High Street with the Tudor gateway on the south-west side of the church front.

Down the years so many urban churches have disappeared – demolished as local populations move out to the suburbs – but Holy Trinity on Gateshead High Street has not only survived successive waves of regeneration but retains all its important architectural features.

The south aisle comprises the thirteenth-century St Edmund's Chapel and was restored for worship by John Dobson in 1837. A splendid frontage of the same period was retained with central doorway and arches and doorways. In about 1247 the chapel became a section of a small hospital which was combined with the hospital of Holy Trinity in 1248.

When Henry VIII's commissioners closed religious houses during the 1530s Holy Trinity was converted into a private house, known as Gateshead House. The impressive Tudor gateway from this property stands on the south-west side of the church front.

In 1893–4 the chapel was enlarged into a new parish church for the growing industrial township but during the twentieth century population shifts brought another change of emphasis. Its position on the High Street made the building an

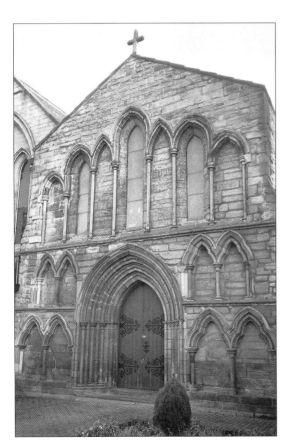

ideal venue for social activity and in 1980, when it was no longer needed as a place of worship, a careful conversion scheme was carried out. Important architectural features were preserved in the restyled building. Part of it continues in use as a church while the other section is used as the Trinity Community Centre.

A VANISHED MANSION AND LINKS WITH EUROPEAN REVOLUTIONARIES

Stella Hall, Blaydon

Access

Stella Hall was demolished in 1953 and the site is now covered by a housing estate (between the B6317 road on the north side and the A695 on the south). Drinking fountains are still in place at Summerhill and Shibden Dene and the bath-house stands in Stella Woods. Stonework of Garibaldi's carved head is on display in the foyer of Blaydon Library and remains of Garibaldi's legs are featured in a flowerpot at St Joseph's Catholic School in Blaydon.

During the second half of the nineteenth century Tyneside had strong links with the European revolutionary leader, Giuseppe Garibaldi, but although he was widely honoured at the time there are few reminders of this colourful character.

GIUSEPPE
GARIBALDI
1807-1882

The initial phase of the struggle for Italian unification was begun by Joseph Mazzini (1805–72) during the early 1840s and from June 1848 he was joined by Giuseppe Garibaldi (1807–82) who had been training a red-shirted Italian Legion in Uruguay to defend republican interests in Montevideo.

One of his staunchest supporters in Britain was Joseph Cowen (1829–1900) who was based at Stella Hall, near the banks of the Tyne at Blaydon. His house had been built in the early seventeenth century by Nicholas Tempest and was purchased by Cowen's father in 1850.

Joseph Cowen was a radical politician with strong principles of Christian democracy and in 1858 he formed the Northern Reform League. Cowen was on friendly terms with a number of European reformers such as Orsini, Mazzini and Kossuth and a number of them, including Garibaldi, were entertained at Stella Hall.

Garibaldi's arrival in Newcastle on 20 March 1854 created considerable interest throughout the area. He arrived as captain of the American cargo ship *The Commonwealth* and some three weeks later, on 11 April 1854, Joseph Cowen handed over a sword of honour and marine telescope. Garibaldi certainly stayed at Stella Hall and tradition suggests that he spent many hours musing about his plans for the Risorgimento movement in Italy at the summerhouse on the Stella Hall estate. (The red-brick octagonal tower on a square rubble base was constructed shortly before 1750 for Sir Thomas Clavering and has fine views over the surrounding countryside.)

During 1860 Garibaldi's forces won dramatic victories in Sicily and Naples before the further stages of Italian unification were engineered by Camillo Cavour (1810–61).

In Britain, Newcastle became England's so-called 'Garibaldian city'. Thoroughfares in central Newcastle and South Shields were named Garibaldi Street and a statue of the area's adopted son was erected at Summerhill on the Stella estate. The statue later toppled over and was broken. The head section was subsequently used as a garden ornament until it was rediscovered and given pride of place in Blaydon Library, while the lower part of the torso forms part of a landscape feature in the grounds of St Joseph's RC School in Blaydon.

On the centenary of Garibaldi's momentous visit, in 1954, an exhibition was staged in Newcastle and during recent years children from Blaydon have participated in exchange visits with Italian youngsters from Pisticci in southern Italy.

Joseph Cowen's daughter, Jane Cowen, lived at Stella until 1946. She left Stella to the University of Durham. It was demolished in 1953 and replaced by a housing estate.

Isolated reminders of the Cowen family's residency at Stella survive in the form of drinking fountains at Summerhill (dated 1860) and at Shibden Dene, along with a bath-house in Stella Woods.

A LANDSCAPED LOCATION WITH MYSTERIOUS STONE STRUCTURE

Friar's Goose

Access

Friar's Goose
stonework
stands within the
East Gateshead
Riverside Park
close to the
Gateshead
Stadium (on the
north side of the
A184).

A puzzling stone structure on the East Gateshead Riverside Park stands in splendid isolation close to Gateshead Stadium. Looking like the remnant of a medieval fortress, it once stood at the heart of a thriving industrial setting where machinery housed within the stonework pumped water from the central seam of the Tyne main colliery. Repair work and refitting was carried out at nearby riverside yards but it was the coal mine and mining families that featured in the so-called 'Battle of Friar's Goose'. During the violent episode in the early days of May 1832 rebellious pitmen and their families were evicted from their cottages.

About one hundred and forty years later, during the early 1970s, the 68-acre site at Friar's Goose was reclaimed at a cost of £110,000, and the lower section of the pumping station now remains in solitary and stately splendour as a reminder of earlier industrial activity.

AN ESTATE OF GLORIOUS SURPRISES

Gibside

At one time the Gibside estate ranked among the finest in the north of England but years of decline and neglect left many of is finest features in a pitiful state. Since the National Trust took over ownership progressive restoration work has uncovered earlier glories and highlighted a number of unusual and unexpected features.

Gibside Hall was built by William Blakiston during the first two decades of the seventeenth century but a hundred years later it passed by marriage to the wealthy Bowes family of Streatlam, near Barnard Castle, and it was George Bowes MP who landscaped adjacent grounds. In 1767 George Bowes' only daughter, Mary, married John Lyon, 9th Earl of Strathmore, and so founded the Bowes-Lyon family. Nine years later the Earl died suddenly and his widow married an unscrupulous adventurer, Andrew Robinson Stoney, who rapidly wasted much of the family wealth before being imprisoned for threatening to kill his wife.

During 1806 the exterior was rebuilt by the 10th Earl of Strathmore, a grandson of George Bowes MP and father of John Bowes, who founded the Bowes Museum at Barnard Castle. A period of disuse saw it fall into disrepair and in 1920 it was dismantled and some of its internal fittings were removed to Glamis Castle. Recent consolidation work has ensured the stability of the

Access

Gibside Estate covers high ground to the east of the River Derwent and is approached via the B6314 from Rowlands Gill (south of the A1 at Blaydon and Whickham via the A694). The estate is owned by the National Trust and entry is subject to normal admission prices and opening times.

structure as it awaits further phases of restoration, while other structures within the estate offer evidence of earlier magnificence.

At the northern end of the Great Walk stands the Column of British Liberty. Towering some 140ft above ground level, the Doric pillar was begun by Daniel Garrett in 1750 but completed between 1753 and 1757 by James Paine. A

symbolic statue on top of the pillar was carved on the site by Christopher Richards of Doncaster and depicts a figure holding the staff of maintenance and cap of liberty. It is regarded as a remarkable representation of eighteenth-century Whig rule.

On the south side of the monument stands Daniel Garrett's Palladian stable block. Built on a square plan around a central courtyard, this fascinating glimpse of eighteenth-century estate life has provided a few surprises during recent restoration work. Conditions in the stables for the horses were of a far better standard than many people enjoyed at the time, and along with fragments of original plaster there were patches of early graffiti (presumably scribbled by stable lads of the time).

The highest point of the park is the location for the Gothic Banqueting House. Designed by Daniel Garrett in 1751, it has many features of an early Gothic Revival

masterpiece (although the plan is essentially Palladian). Restoration work was carried out during 1980 and it is now under the ownership of the Landmark Trust. At the foot of the slope below the Banqueting House the Octagon Pond remains undisturbed as it has become a haven for insect and plant life.

Other features on the Gibside estate include a late eighteenth-century ice house and an orangery from the same period. The chapel and mausoleum was begun in 1760 for George Bowes MP and his instructions to the designer James Paine specified that it should be completed within six years of his death. Work on the interior stopped in 1769, several years after Bowes' death, and it was only after the 10th Earl had completed the project in 1812 that George Bowes was buried in the underfloor mausoleum.

With its central altar, stately three-decker pulpit topped by a rare umbrella-shaped sounding board and large box pews (with curved seats for servants and

visitors and corner sections for the owner, agent and chaplain), it represents a fine example of a Georgian church in the most superior classical style. It attracts even more interest and is seen as important because the chapel represents James Paine's only free-standing church building.

An unusual surprise awaited landscape gardeners when areas of the estate were recently being replanted. Earlier gardeners had placed slabs of stone below ground level in order to force tree roots to grow out wide and reduce their height.

DELIGHTFUL SETTING FOR A VARIETY OF TANTALISING FEATURES

Ryton

Access

Ryton village lies
to the north of
the B6317 on
sloping ground
running downhill
by the River
Tyne.

Ryton's strategic position at the lowest fording point across the Tyne resulted in frequent clashes during the years of border warfare but in more recent times low land beside the river has been used as an area for recreation. Boating parties arrived from Newcastle at the ferry landing where roundabouts and all the fun of the fairground spread along the low ground of Ryton Willows.

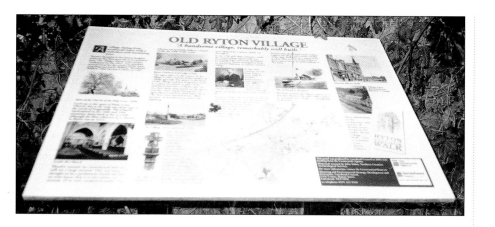

Looking down on this lowland setting is the Church of the Holy Cross. The earliest parts of the building date from the thirteenth century but it has been modernised in the eighteenth and nineteenth centuries. The unusual lead-covered spire which rises 120ft above the churchyard is the only one of its kind in the north of England. A large mound in the adjacent churchyard was at one time thought to be the site of a prehistoric burial but recent investigations indicate that it was in fact the motte of an early medieval castle. (The earliest church building probably originated as a chapel for the castle.)

There is reference to a pinfold at Ryton in the twelfth century. Many villages had a walled enclosure where stray animals could be impounded and then claimed by their owners on payment of a small fee but Ryton's pinfold is unusual because animals were watered by a central stream that ran through the sloping pen. This splendid stone structure was restored by Ryton Heritage Group in 1974. A nearby ornamental fountain adds further interest to this charming location.

Newcastle Curling Club played their last official match on Ryton Willows at the beginning of the Second World War but it seems that some of the dips and hollows on this level expanse of riverside land were created as wartime measures. Anti-aircraft sites were based here and parallel rows of square pits and mounds are thought to represent aircraft obstruction ditches. Running from north to south across the Willows, they were intended to prevent enemy gliders or troop-carrying aircraft from landing in the event of an invasion.

A GEM OF EARLY RAILWAY ARCHITECTURE

Brandling Station

Access

Brandling station is adjacent to Mulberry Street in Felling (on the north side of the Metro station which is close to the B1426).

Tyneside's role in early railway development is well documented and a fascinating survival from those pioneering days is to be found close to the modern Metro station at Felling. The Brandling Junction Railway derives its name from R.W. Brandling and his brother John, who planned to connect Monkwearmouth with South Shields and Gateshead. An act of parliament incorporated the company on 7 June 1836 and sections of the line opened in three stages during 1839.

The curious little Gothic-style railway station opened in 1842 alongside Mulberry Street in Felling and a 'BR' tablet set in the stonework refers to the Brandling Railway. Following closure in 1869 the building fell into a state of disrepair but restoration work during 1978 saw it brought into use as an urban studies centre. A plaque on the north wall refers to its importance as one of the oldest passenger stations in England.

MODERN SCULPTURE ON THE GRAND SCALE

The Angel of the North

During the 1990s Gateshead developed a Public Art Programme with innovative works throughout the town, but the most dramatic element of the scheme must be the *Angel of the North*. Created by Antony Gormley and composed of 196 tons of steel, it is anchored to the elevated site of a former colliery pithead baths by massive concrete piles some 65ft deep. Sections of the *Angel* measuring up to 65ft wide and 82ft long were assembled in Hartlepool and transported to their position at the head of the Team Valley in February 1998.

Standing some 65ft high and with a wingspan of 177ft it is believed to be the largest angel sculpture in the world, and is certainly one of the most viewed pieces of artwork. The *Angel* towers over the A1 from where it is viewed by over 90,000 drivers a day or more than one a second – and it is also clearly seen by passengers on the East Coast Main Line between London and Edinburgh. Capable of withstanding winds of more than 100 miles per hour it is expected to remain in place for over 100 years.

The *Angel*'s rusty red-brown colour has resulted from the use of weather-resistant steel which contains copper. As the surface oxidises a patina is formed and this results in the mellow brown coating.

Love it or loathe it, the *Angel of the North* continues to provoke an endless amount of interest and comment.

Access

The *Angel of the North* is seen by multitudes of motorists on the A1 while pedestrian access to the base of the sculpture is from the A167 on the east side.

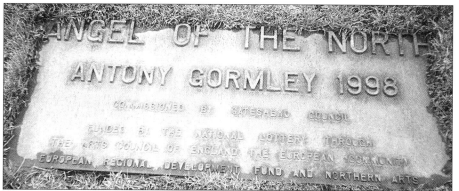

A PUZZLING TOWER

King George's Field, Whickham

Access

The windmill at Whickham stands in a central position at the southern end of Chase Park between Rectory Lane (to the west) and Broom Lane (on the east side).

The circular tower which stands on high ground in King George's Field (Chase Park) could easily be taken for a beacon or lookout tower. Then again, it could possibly have been a base for a gun battery or even a ventilation shaft for underground workings in the area. In fact, it was a windmill made of materials from several different periods.

One of the lintels has the date '1567' and it seems that upper millstones were broken up or buried as the Scottish Parliamentary Army advanced on Whickham in 1640. Newspaper references in 1806 point to a phase of rebuilding in 1720 while upper courses of stonework seem to date from the twentieth century and are straighter than the slightly sloped lower section.

A TEMPERANCE OASIS

Law's Herbal Supplies

Central Gateshead has seen several phases of redevelopment in recent years but a retail business at the southern end of the High Street represents a throwback to much earlier days. Law's Herbal Supplies has been run by the same family for the last 160 years and must rank as one of the few remaining temperance bars.

During the second half of the nineteenth century temperance bars were opened throughout the country in an attempt to counter the tide of alcohol abuse, but most closed long ago. Law's survived and continues to sell herbal products such as sarsaparilla for consumption on the premises or to take away.

Appropriately, perhaps, Law's premises are located next door to one of Gateshead's town centre bars and with further plans for redevelopment of this sector of the High Street it seems that days are numbered for this unusual temperance outlet.

Access

Law's Herbal Supplies is located at the southern end of Gateshead High Street (west side) in an area of the town centre which is scheduled for redevelopment.

SPARSE REMAINS OF AN AMAZING MEDIEVAL-STYLE CASTLE

Ravensworth Castle

Access

Ravensworth
Castle is
surrounded by
farmland on the
west side of the
A1 (opposite the
Team Valley
Trading Estate).
Public roads run
along each side
of the
Ravensworth
area but the land
itself is privately
owned and not
accessible.

A castle existed at Ravensworth from the twelfth century but its buildings were small in scale and simple in design. The Liddell family added a large but modest residence inside the castle precincts during the 1720s with additional details some thirty years later.

In 1808 the architect John Nash drew up designs for a new home with Gothic exterior and classical interiors but building work seems to have continued under Thomas Henry Liddell up to 1840. The arrangement of battlemented walls, towers and turrets represented one of the finest romantic medieval revivals in the north-east of England. Arcades, tall arched alcoves and a hammer beam roof characterised the Great Hall while fan vaulting and Gothic lanterns featured in the Long Gallery.

Following the death of the 5th Lord Ravensworth in 1919, furniture, books and paintings were sold and the castle became a girls' school. The 7th Baron inherited the property in 1932 and announced plans to demolish the castle and build a model village. In the face of widespread opposition to his scheme Lord Ravensworth disclosed that a 30-acre coalfield had undermined the buildings and

caused serious weakening of walls and foundations. He died in 1950 before redevelopment got under way but his successor engineered demolition in 1953.

Although the main buildings were cleared away, parts of the stables remain along with a castellated gateway, south lodge and half-timbered structure. Along with a tall stone column known as Butler Cross they provide a tantalising reminder of Ravensworth's romantic castle.

A WHIMSICAL MANSION AMONG A COLLECTION OF ODDITIES

Saltwell Park

During the second half of the nineteenth century southern sectors of Gateshead were developed with large properties set in extensive parkland. Most notable of these was the 58-acre Saltwell Park where a Tyneside glass manufacturer, William Wailes, set up home in a truly whimsical residence. Built during the 1860s with red brickwork highlighted by yellow and black pattern work, the mansion has a

Access

Saltwell Park spreads along sloping ground on the west side of the A167 in central Gateshead, south of the town's technical college. The park is subject to normal opening times arranged by Gateshead Council.

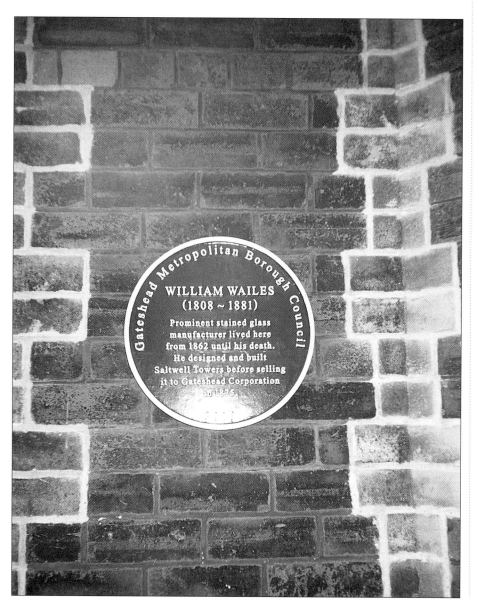

romantic skyline of soaring turrets, chimneys and battlements. Internal rooms were fitted out with a whole range of extravagant fittings and furniture.

Surrounding parkland was landscaped for public use in 1877 by W.B. Kemp from Birkenhead with an expanse of lawn sweeping down to a large lake. Original features included a long terrace of flowers, a secluded sunken rose garden and a hedged enclosure with an open-air draughtboard. A kiosk from the North East Coast Exhibition in Newcastle was removed to Saltwell Park for use as a rest room in 1929 and in the postwar years the fine nineteenth-century mansion was used as a local and industrial museum.

Although the parkland was still popular with local folk, decline set in and the house and surrounding features lapsed into a sorry state during the later years of the twentieth century. A major restoration scheme in the early twenty-first century has seen the reopening of Saltwell Towers as a visitors' centre and café with space for exhibitions and special events. The surrounding parkland has a range of areas for different outdoor events and the replanting of William Wailes' original maze along with restoration of the Almond Pavilion to its original appearance of 1881 have helped to recreate the atmosphere of the late nineteenth century. During refurbishment of a temperance fountain at the lower end of the Dene a lower basin was uncovered. It supplied water for dogs and was labelled with the phrase 'for ye goode of thirstie dogges'.

A GIANT OF A MAN
WITH A HUGE REPUTATION

Long Jack English

In earlier days many areas boasted a local 'strongman', a mighty fellow with incredible strength and an inflated reputation. During the first half of the nineteenth century the exploits of John English were the talk of Tyneside's taverns and tea-rooms.

John English was born in about 1800 at Chester-le-Street and moved to the Whickham area in 1830 to work as a stonemason on the Scotswood Bridge. Standing 6ft 4½in tall, his skills were in great demand, but he still found time to build his own house at the end of Woodhouse Lane. Reports indicate that he

moved stone for the house on his own using a bogey and also man-handled chimney tops that weighed 1½cwt each from Blaydon Bank quarry some 4½ miles away.

During his working life English fashioned pillars for the old Butterfly Bridge across the River Derwent at the bottom of Clockburn Lane and in 1848 he worked on the project to renovate Lamesley Church.

As tales of his exploits spread around the neighbourhood so John English's reputation assumed almost legendary proportions. His party piece at weekend gatherings was to jump in the air and smash a hole in the ceiling with his head, and after his dog had been run over by a wagon he is said to have picked up the wagon with its load of stones and then tipped it on its side along with the horse that was pulling it.

John English became a local celebrity and led processions at the head of religious or political meetings. In 1854 an 18ft-high statue was erected opposite the English family's home. A local sculptor, John Norvell, carved the head and shoulders on the upper section of the stone column some six years before John English's death in 1860.

The monument was damaged at a later date and following repair work it was moved to a central position in the village. An inscription on the column states 'MCMLXXVI. Donated by Bellway to Whickham Village.' This monument formerly stood in Woodhouses Lane Fellside. The adjacent public house which was formerly named the Rose and Crown has been renamed Ye Olde Lang Jack.

BATTERED, BURNT OUT AND RECENTLY REBORN

St Mary's Church

Access

St Mary's church building – now Gateshead Visitor Centre – is a landmark on high ground close to the Tyne Bridge and adjacent to the Sage.

From its lofty position on the banks of the Tyne, St Mary's Church has dominated the skyline of downtown Gateshead for centuries. Most of this fine building dates from the fourteenth century although the west tower was added in the eighteenth century and down the years it has withstood a whole series of destructive episodes.

Earlier buildings on the site were wrecked in 1080 when Bishop Watcher was murdered and his church destroyed. During the following centuries, care and support for the local community was provided through a school and poorhouse within the church precincts but these services must have been interrupted by events in the English Civil War.

During the midsummer of 1644 Royalist supporters were attacked by Parliamentary troops at a location known as Windmill Hill (on the south side of St Mary's) and after being decisively defeated the King's forces fled across the

98

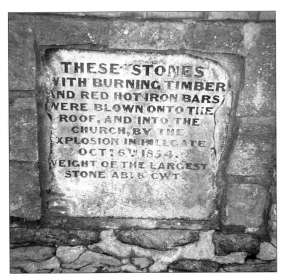

river to Newcastle. By 22 July five gun batteries had been installed on Windmill Hill in order to direct cannon fire at Newcastle while Scottish troops were based within the walls of St Mary's Church. Hostilities lasted for about three weeks during which St Mary's was damaged by fire from both sides of the river (and by occupying troops) before Newcastle was captured by Parliamentary forces.

Disaster struck both banks of the Tyne in the early hours of 6 October 1854 when fire broke out on Newcastle Quayside. Flames soon spread from the seven-storey Bertrams Warehouse to a nearby chemical works and in the resulting explosions rocks and debris showered down on St Mary's Church.

Construction of the Tyne Bridge between 1925 and 1928 saw removal of large areas of the churchyard and adjacent grounds but St Mary's continued at the heart of the Anglican community in Gateshead until fire broke out on 19 October 1979. For the next ten years it remained as an eyesore, empty and unused as successive plans for conversion into flats, a shopping centre, charity centre and restaurant failed to materialise.

It finally returned to use after restoration work had been carried out by the Civic Trust in the late 1980s. Phillips Fine Art Auctioneers purchased the church and converted it into an auction house with the addition of an interior mezzanine floor and car park. The building's future was finally safeguarded in 2003 when Gateshead Council purchased St Mary's with assistance from the Heritage Lottery Fund. Further adaptations saw the church re-styled as a visitor centre with tourist information facilities and crafts gallery.

Faced with destruction on countless occasions St Mary's has finally experienced a remarkable renaissance.

A MASSIVE MONUMENT TO THE HEYDAY OF 'KING COAL'

Dunston Staithes

The south bank of the Tyne has a striking monument to this area's coal-mining heyday in the form of Dunston Staithes. Dating from 1893, they were constructed on ground previously covered by seventeenth-century staithes that had handled coal supplies transported from Whickham Colliery along wagonways.

Standing some 43ft above high water mark, this amazing timber structure measured around 558 yards in length and during its peak period a total of 100,000 tons of coal could be loaded each month. Railway lines ran across an enormous framework to load up to six colliers at any one time and the staithes represented a crucial aspect of the coal industry. With a large workforce engaged in aspects of the operation the nearby settlement of Dunston became almost entirely a keelmen's village.

Dunston Staithes closed in 1980 but they were restored as part of the National Garden Festival during 1990.

Access

Dunston Staithes dominate the river frontage between the High Level Bridge and the Metro Centre.

CONCRETE CURIOSITY OR SOARING MONSTROSITY?

Access

The multi-storey
car park
dominates the
eastern side of
Gateshead's
central shopping
area between
West Street and
the High Street.

A thirteen-storey car park in the centre of Gateshead

The centre of Gateshead is dominated by a thirteen-storey car park that has created controversy and debate since its opening on 1 August 1969. Designed by the architect Owen Luder, it was constructed at a cost of £200,000 and was said by planners at the time to 'herald the start of a new era in the development of Gateshead's shopping'.

During the early months of 1971 shallow mine workings under the car park led to an eight-week-long programme of strengthening work and in the late 1970s plans for a rooftop nightclub were abandoned. Proposals for a Sunday second-hand car market were also rejected in 1980 but it was the film *Get Carter* (1971) that gave the car park world-wide exposure. (Michael Caine starred in the movie as a vengeful London gangster pursuing his brother's killers at various locations in the north-east.)

In 1999 the structure was becoming an unsafe eyesore and approval was given for demolition. Readers of the local newspaper, the *Evening Chronicle*, voted the car park as the region's ugliest landmark. Members of the 'Get Carter Appreciation Society' promptly announced plans to send a piece of concrete from the car park to Sir Michael Caine and claimed that this 1960s edifice would be sadly missed.

In late 2006 the car park's future remains undecided.

3

CURIOSITIES
OF NORTH TYNESIDE

DEFENCE AGAINST INVASION BY DUTCH FORCES

Clifford's Fort

Access

Clifford's Fort is partially hidden by adjacent buildings close to North Shields Fish Quay. Nearby High and Low Lights form interesting landmarks that merit a closer look.

Tucked away among the warehouses and sheds around North Shields Fish Quay is a relic from the days when Tynesiders went in fear of invasion by Dutch forces. Clifford's Fort was constructed in 1672 at a time when England was at war with Holland; it housed artillery pieces with a line of fire covering the mouth of the Tyne.

Since those times parts of the outer walls have been removed but a plaque on a southern section of brickwork explains that the fort was named after Lord Clifford of Cabal and that it was initially armed with twenty 20-pounder and ten 10-pounder cannons. It was under the command of the Governor of Tynemouth Castle until 1839 and later in the century, when fear of invasion again increased, Clifford's Fort became the headquarters of the Tyne Division Royal Engineers (Volunteers) Submarine Miners (between 1888 and 1928).

Though upper sections of the outer walls have been removed it is still possible to trace a hole in the wall for directing artillery fire and the remains of sheds where mines were assembled and fitted with fuses.

NORTH TYNESIDE COUNCIL

CLIFFORD'S FORT

Completed in 1672 and named after Lord Clifford of Cabal, this fort was first armed with 20 x 20 pdr and ten x 10 pdr cannons.

Commanded by Governor of Tynemouth Castle until 1839.

Headquarters of Tyne Division Royal Engineers (Volunteers) Submarine Miners 1888–1928.

1990

SIDE BY SIDE

Hotel and House of Correction

In recent years large sectors of North Shields have been redeveloped but at locations such as Correction House Bank buildings have survived to provide fascinating glimpses of earlier days.

A plaque on the front wall of the Tynemouth Lodge Hotel states that the premises have operated as a public house and residential hotel since 1799. Further details explain that meals for prisoners in the adjoining House of Correction

Access

The House of Correction and Tynemouth Lodge Hotel line the west side of Tynemouth Road close to the boundary with North Shields.

(built 1792) were prepared in the cellar kitchen of the hotel and delivered through an underground tunnel to inmates and court officials in the adjacent Justice Room.

From 1907 the splendidly named House of Correction served as the Tynemouth and District Laundry, and although a modern frontage has been added to a part of the building which now houses an Archaeological Salvage Company, there are echoes within its walls of earlier days when justice was meted out to wrong-doers.

A LINGERING LINK
WITH THE SECOND WORLD WAR

Pillbox, Preston Cemetery

Access

Remnants of the wartime pillbox are built into a roadside wall on the north-east side of Preston cemetery.

Until recent years pillboxes were a common sight at strategically important locations throughout Britain. Concrete blockhouses represented an integral part of defences against invading forces but in the face of redevelopment schemes and safety considerations, many have been removed.

Strangely, one pillbox that has survived is to be found beside the roadway on the north-east side of Preston cemetery. Fashioned from a section of brick wall, it is now boxed in by modern properties and despite this incongruous setting it represents a rare survival in a built-up area.

A TOWERING RELIC
FROM FIRST WORLD WAR DAYS

The Command Centre

Access

The landmark command centre peeps above rooftops at the northern end of Percy Gardens, Tynemouth, and is privately owned.

Looming over rooftops at the northern end of Tynemouth's Percy Gardens is a relic from the days when fear of invasion by enemy forces loomed large. Built in about 1913 the white-painted command centre covered a central area between similar watchtowers at Roberts Battery at Hartley to the north and the Kitchener Battery at Marsden, further south.

This Grade II Listed concrete structure stands six storeys high with windows offering views across the North Sea and although alterations were made, original window fittings have since been installed. Representing an unusual throwback to anxious times before the First World War, the lookout post is now privately owned.

MILITARY AND MONASTIC RUINS

Tynemouth Castle and Priory

Access

Tynemouth
Castle and Priory
cover high
ground
overlooking the
mouth of the
river and the
north pier.

North-east England has an impressive collection of castles and monastic houses, with many of them located along the North Sea coastline. It is highly unusual to find the stonework of castle and priory standing side by side but on the sandstone headland at Tynemouth a set of strident military works contrast markedly with the sedate priory ruins.

For more than 1,300 years monastic buildings of some description have stood on this headland which is surrounded on three sides by North Sea breakers. Early church buildings were repeatedly devastated by Danish raiders during the late eighth century AD and for more than 100 years the priory remained deserted. During the reign of Edward the Confessor, in the mid-eleventh century, Earl Tostig, brother of Harold of Wessex, established a military base on the headland but he died at the Battle of Stamford Bridge (1066) before he could re-found the monastery.

The priory was rebuilt in about 1100 and just a few years earlier, in 1095, Robert de Mowbray's castle on the headland had been captured by royal forces. The site's strategic importance meant that military and religious claims to the location often led to disputes.

Ownership of the priory was disputed by the Abbey of St Albans and Durham Cathedral. The Mowbray family had granted Tynemouth to St Albans but the long-running dispute was only resolved in their favour in 1174, and it seems that they used it primarily as a place of exile for recalcitrant monks.

During the thirteenth century the church building was almost doubled in length and a range of farm buildings on the north side supplied the household's food rations. Raids by Scottish forces caused shortages and after a visit by King Edward I in 1297 defences around the site were strengthened. A substantial

gatehouse was constructed and raiding parties led by Gilbert de Middleton were resisted during 1317.

Supplies to this clifftop stronghold could be brought in via Prior's Haven, a cove at the foot of the headland, but landward defences needed further strengthening in the late fourteenth century and the barbican was rebuilt at this time.

The closure of the priory in 1539 allowed priory lands and areas of the castle to be used for local defences. Positions in front of the gatehouse were bolstered and gun emplacements beside Prior's Haven were manned for a while by Spanish mercenaries.

During the late sixteenth and early seventeenth centuries the castle buildings were neglected but Tynemouth's strategic importance saw the castle's defences restored during the period of the Civil War. In 1660 Captain Villiers was appointed captain of Tynemouth Castle and subsequent years saw the conversion of monastic buildings to military use.

The graveyard close to the ruined church includes a headstone of Corporal Alexander Rollo of the Royal Artillery, who died in 1856, aged eighty-two. His claim to fame was that he held the lantern at the burial of Sir John Moore at Corunna in 1809. The same burial ground was also the final resting place for two early warrior kings. Both Oswin of Deira (in about 651) and Osred of Northumbria (in 792) were murdered during turbulent pre-conquest days and these burials seem to serve as a reminder of this remote headland's combined role as a monastic centre and strategic stronghold.

A SERIES OF WOODEN DOLLIES AT NORTH SHIELDS

Custom House Quay

Access

The wooden dolly is located at the centre of Northumberland Square, North Shields.

North Shields' origins date back to the early thirteenth century when the cluster of riverside huts (or shiels) was linked to the nearby Tynemouth Priory. In more recent years the town's connections with ships and the fishing industry have been celebrated by a series of carved 'wooden dollies'.

The first wooden dolly took the form of a figurehead from the coal ship *Alexander and Margaret* which Alexander Bartleman and his wife Margaret sited in the front garden of their home at 23 Front Street, Tynemouth, in about 1814. It was placed there in honour of their son, David, who was fatally injured during naval action against the French, but a move to Custom House Quay at North Shields soon brought about the dolly's demise. Mooring ropes were wrapped around the base and local vandals caused further damage before a group of revellers completed the destruction of this original dolly in about 1850.

A second dolly was soon installed at the same position on the quay by a local sailmaker, Mr Hare, but lasted little more than a dozen years before it was replaced by another figurehead on 23 June 1864. Again the wooden dolly suffered ill treatment as sailors nailed coins into it to bring good luck and even a replacement iron nose could not prolong its time on the quay beyond the early months of the twentieth century.

The fourth wooden dolly brought a changed appearance. Carved by Miss Mary Spence, it was unveiled on Coronation Day, 26 June 1902, and represented a fishwife carrying a creel on her back. This dolly lasted well into the 1950s before it was replaced by a mahogany figure carved in the workshop of Robert Thompson Ltd, at Kilburn in North Yorkshire. It was unveiled by the town's mayor, Leonard G. Dolby, in 1958 and occupies a central position in Northumberland Square.

An additional wooden dolly, a replica of the third, was installed on Custom House Quay in October 1992 outside the Prince of Wales Tavern. It is carved from a section of oak at a cost of £5,000 and weighs 1½ tons.

A STATUE BY TWO SCULPTORS

The Duke of Northumberland, Tynemouth

The influence of the Duke of Northumberland is apparent at many locations on the north side of the River Tyne and a splendid statue of a robed duke occupies a central position on the forecourt of the Master Mariners' Homes at Tynemouth.

Access

The statue of the Duke of Northumberland in front of the Master Mariners' Homes overlooks Tynemouth Road.

The statue was unveiled on 11 September 1937 and holds particular interest because the monument was begun by the sculptor Christopher Tate. Sadly he died before the work was complete and it was left to another sculptor, R.G. Davies, to finish the impressive statue. Christopher Tate (1812–41) showed outstanding talent as a sculptor during his apprenticeship under R.G. Davies and then as assistant to David Dunbar. His early work was exhibited at the Royal Academy and was described by the *Gentleman's Magazine* as 'exceptional'. One of his best-known works was *Blind Willie* and he also fashioned a coat of arms that was displayed on Newcastle's Theatre Royal.

The line of Tudor-style sandstone properties behind the statue was completed during the late 1830s.

4

CURIOSITIES
OF SOUTH TYNESIDE

CONTRASTING MONUMENTS IN HONOUR OF THREE LOCAL HEROES

Wounded soldier Private Kirkpatrick and two pioneering boat builders, William Wouldhave and Henry Greathead

Access

The Kirkpatrick statue stands in a central position on Ocean Road, South Shields, close to the junction with King Street.

The South Tyneside area has a whole range of sculptures including a number of contemporary design pieces that are sure to intrigue and fascinate – but it is a duo of traditional monuments that have a truly dramatic impact.

A bronze statue in the centre of South Shields is the work of Bertram Pegram and shows a wounded soldier riding a donkey on the battlefield at Gallipoli during the First World War. The casualty is supported by Private John Simpson Kirkpatrick of the Australian Medical Corps, who was born in South Shields. For more than five weeks during the Gallipoli campaign, Private Kirkpatrick and his donkey spent long periods retrieving wounded soldiers from the battlefield. Often they were faced with heavy rifle and machine-gun fire and on 19 May 1915 Kirkpatrick was cut down by enemy fire after completing four journeys down Shrapnel Gulley, the most deadly sector of the peninsula.

At the eastern end of Ocean Road in South Shields stands a dramatic reminder of two local men who constructed the first practical lifeboat. A tall stone-built clock tower has panels showing the two pioneering boat builders, William Wouldhave and Henry Greathead, and another tablet illustrates a lifeboat heading towards a wrecked vessel in the teeth of a raging storm.

A London-based coach builder named Lionel Lukin developed a lifeboat during 1785 but serious structural weaknesses meant that it was soon abandoned. Four years later, in 1789, a vessel named *The Adventure* was wrecked on the Herd Sands at the mouth of the River Tyne. Watchers on the shore were unable to help as crew members were swept to their death and following the tragedy local people began to organise a voluntary lifeboat service. A prize was offered for a boat which could put to sea in

Access

The lifeboat
memorial is at
the eastern end
of Ocean Road
close to the Pier
Park and South
Marine Park.

storm conditions and William Wouldhave constructed a model which was improved by Henry Greathead.

Greathead's specialist knowledge of boat building led him to suggest that Wouldhave's model should have a curved keel, rather than a straight one. The completed lifeboat measured 30ft in length and had a width of 10ft with layers of cork on the inside and outside. Power was in the hands of ten oarsmen and there was space on board for twenty people. The total cost of £149 13*s* 9*d* was met by the Committee of the Coal Trade in Newcastle, and during years of service the lifeboat saved hundreds of stranded mariners.

Alongside the clock tower a canopy shelters a lifeboat which dates from 1833 and was instrumental in saving over 1,000 lives. A nearby anchor is believed to have come from a wrecked Spanish galleon and was retrieved from the North Sea by a trawler in 1920.

FLAMBOYANT EXTRAVAGANZA OF BRICKWORK AND TERRACOTTA

Red Cottage

Access

Red Cottage stands beside the roadway on Church Lane at Cleadon, a few yards south of the parish church.

Rows of Georgian properties line both sides of Front Street in Whitburn village and large villas around the bank, on the north side, have special appeal. On the opposite side of the strip of central grassland Church Lane leads to St Andrew's Church, the former rectory and an extraordinary example of patterned brickwork at Red Cottage.

Designed by Benjamin Green, it was built for the brickworks owner Thomas Barnes during 1842–3 and represents an early example of highly decorative brickwork. Almost every section of the building from crowstep gables to moulded Tudor-style chimneystacks has been embellished by some form of pattern work. The flat-topped peak of each gable displays a ball or stump which was added by a later owner with a strong interest in the game of cricket.

A CLIFF FACE CURIOSITY

Marsden's White Horse

Access

The white horse
is painted on a
north-facing cliff
above housing
on the northern
edge of Cleadon.
It is visible from
Prince Edward
Road, South
Shields. The
public house is a
few hundred
yards west along
the bridleway.

Up and down the British mainland there are several examples of hill figures. Most date from the eighteenth and nineteenth centuries and some, such as Kilburn's white horse (created in 1857) on the Hambleton Hills in North Yorkshire, can be spotted from a considerable distance. Often the background to these landscape features is well documented but no one knows for sure who carved the outline of a horse on the limestone cliff face of a quarry at Marsden near South Shields.

While not as prominent as its better-known counterparts, Marsden's white horse has nevertheless attracted any number of assorted legends. One tale harks back to the days of Viking raids and the death in battle of a Scandinavian warlord. Following a fierce battle in which everyone was massacred, the chieftain's loyal stallion is said to have wandered around the area in search of its lost master.

During more recent times a persistent story suggests that the white horse was in fact a highly valued wild mare that was owned by a Victorian horse trainer. A farm worker called William Johnstone is said to have disobeyed instructions and tried to break the horse. He was unseated and badly injured as he tumbled into the quarry.

Disabled by his injuries, Johnstone was unable to walk again and one storyline states that his children started the tradition of depicting the horse at the location of his fateful fall. Regular repaintings of the white horse took place in the years

that followed and the rather larger image is said to have been the work of soldiers who were based in the area throughout the First World War.

A reminder of the location's puzzling painting is provided by a nearby public house which is suitably named the White Horse.

ICE HOUSE, BOATHOUSE OR NEITHER?

Cleadon Garden Grotto

Access

At the north-western edge of Coulthard Park (known locally as Bluebell Park) close to the centre of Cleadon.

An element of mystery surrounds the strange brick-built structure at the northern end of the village park close to the centre of Cleadon Village. Almost prison-like in appearance with bars covering the line of arches along its frontage, it is half-covered by an earth embankment and faces the area of open ground that was originally covered by an ornamental lake. Some reports state that pleasure boats were housed underneath the arches in readiness for launching on the lake while other references are made to the structure's use as an ice house.

A plaque on the upper wall refers to this puzzling pile as 'an 18th century garden ornament . . . in the grounds of Cleadon House'. It was repaired by the Borough of South Tyneside as a contribution to the Cleadon 800 Festival in 1983.

THE SPLENDID, SILENT
CONVERSATION PIECE

Harbour Drive, South Shields

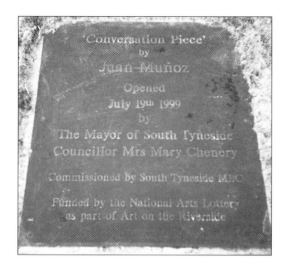

Access

Spreads around
an area of the
promenade
(A183) towards
the Groyne and
South Pier.

The Art on the Riverside project is composed of more than 100 varied artworks around the area of Tyne & Wear and one of the most impressive of these has to be *The Conversation Piece* which is located at the north end of the B1344 Harbour Drive, South Shields.

This collection of twenty-two bronze figures weighing about ¼ ton each was created by the Spanish sculptor, Juan Muñoz, during 1999, and serves as a reminder of the range of

languages spoken by local immigrants and sea-going men from Celts, Romans and Vikings to Arabs and Asians.

Sadly, Muñoz died at the peak of his creative output in 2001 but *The Conversation Piece*, which is affectionately known by local folk as 'The Weebles', represents an enduring and intriguing representation of his splendid craftsmanship.

A UNIQUE LOCAL CHARACTER

Dolly Peel

Access

Dolly Peel stands on a raised grassy bank near the bridge on River Drive facing the river frontage and North Sea.

Every area has a unique collection of local characters who have made a mark in their chosen walk of life. More often than not these individuals were men and many left their local neighbourhood in search of fame and fortune, but one notable exception was Dolly Peel, whose exploits saw her firmly established in the folklore of the South Shields area.

Born in 1782, Dolly worked as a fishwife but she also belonged to the local smuggling fraternity and helped to distribute illicit cargoes of items such as brandy, tobacco, lace, cigars and perfume. For a time she served in the Royal Navy but back on home ground she took a stand against forays by press gangs and attracted large crowds to the town's marketplace to hear her humorous speeches. There was even time for her to write poems championing the cause of Robert Ingham, South Shields' first Member of Parliament.

Dolly Peel died in 1857 but her fascinating life has been celebrated in many different formats. In addition to a photograph dating from about 1850 there are at least five oil paintings of Dolly and in 1923 she was the central character in a play that was performed locally. During 1995 local college students and actors produced a video, *Dolly Peel*, and ten years later a musical with the same title was performed at local venues.

An enduring reminder of Dolly Peel and her intriguing life took shape in 1987. It takes the form of a statue fashioned by Bill Gofton and stands on an open grassy area close to River Drive and Palatine Street at South Shields. The full-length figure of Dolly faces the busy downtown area close to the River Tyne, a setting where she spent much of her sparkling lifetime.

MARSDEN GROTTO

Marsden Bay

Access

Coastal position
beside the A183
just south of
South Shields.

England's north-east coastline has any number of interesting locations but one of the most bewitching settings is to be found at Marsden Bay where the Grotto has provided a base for a host of colourful characters. Constant battering by North Sea breakers has carved a series of caves along this stretch of coast and the first person known to have made a home at Marsden was 'Jack the Blaster'. He originally came from Allenheads but found work at a local quarry and based himself in caves at Marsden during 1782. A long flight of stairs that led down to caves near Marsden Rock were said to have been hacked from the cliffs by Jack himself and it was here that he mixed smuggling and poaching with work at the

quarry. Fashionable members of society were drawn to Marsden Grotto where Jack and his wife served refreshments and began the tradition of hospitality.

During the 1830s the caverns at Marsden Grotto were occupied by Peter Allan who had worked locally as a valet, gamekeeper and construction worker. An increasing number of visitors were being drawn to the natural attractions at Marsden Bay and Peter Allan improved facilities by enlarging the caverns to include a bar, ballroom and living rooms. He even drilled a shaft through the ceiling of one of the largest caves in order to allow supplies to be lowered from the cliff top into the living quarters. The extremes of winter weather caused problems for the Allan family with gigantic waves surging into the caves, and during winter 1846 the whole area around Marsden Bay was blocked for about six weeks. Peter Allan and his family survived and in calmer weather this remarkable character, assisted by two workmen, constructed a series of ladders from the shore to the summit of Marsden Rock which stood some 109ft high. He reared a whole collection of animals including pigs, bees, doves and a tame raven named Ralph up to his death in 1850.

The sense of mystery at Marsden deepened with the discovery of a skeleton of a tall man some 3ft below the surface in 1836. Other excavations uncovered several more skeletons while smuggling tales have provided stories of hauntings by a character known as 'John the Jibber'.

A massive rock fall during 1865 destroyed sections of the Grotto but extensive repairs were carried out by the Allan family before their connection with this remote shoreline setting ended in 1874. During 1898 Messrs Vaux & Co. Ltd took over the lease of Marsden Grotto and some forty years later they purchased the premises. Since then the facilities have been modernised but this fascinating location has lost none of its interest and appeal.

INDEX

Allan, Peter 124
All Hallows 36
All Saints' Church 36–7
Amen Corner 39
Angel of the North 52, 85
Anglican Old Catholic Church of St
    Willibrord 36
Armstrong, Lord 29
Armstrong-Whitworth 64

Ballast Hills 27
Balliol, Edward 34
Balmbra's (Reflex) 20–1
Baltic Centre for Contemporary Art 57
Barley Mow Estate 64
Barnes, Thomas 117
Bell, Leah 21
Betjeman, Sir John 36
Bewick, Thomas 67
Birtley 64
Blackett, Sir Walter 32
Blackett Place 40
Blackett Street 40
Blackfriars 34–5
Blackshields, Scotland 32
Blakiston, William 75
Blaydon Races 21
Blaydon Urban District Council 21
Blythe's Pillar 60
Bowes, George 75, 78
Bowes, John 75
Brandling station 84
Byker Bridge 15
Byker Viaduct 26
Byker Wall 14–17

Caine, Sir Michael 100
Cawley, Revd John 28
Chester-le-Street 94
Chinatown 42
Chinese Arch 42
Clasper, Henry 62
Clasper, Jane 62
Clavering House 31

Clifford's Fort 102
Cole, Richard 58–9
Cowen, Jane 73
Cowen, Joseph 72
Crawford's Bridge 24
Crawford's Row 24
Crown Posada 18

Derwenthaugh 62
Dobson, John 68
Dunston Staithes 99

Edward I, King 108
Edward III, King 29, 34
Elisabethville 63
English, John 94–5
Erskine, Ralph 15

Foster, Lord Norman 55
Friar's Goose 74

Gallipoli 114
Garibaldi, Giuseppe 70
Garden Grotto, Cleaden 120
Gateshead, Central Hotel 65
    Council 52
    Multi-storey car park 100
    Old Post Office 66–7
    Quays 53, 55
    Shipley Art Gallery 61
    Stadium 74
    Trinity Community Centre 68
Get Carter (1971) 100
Gibside 75–9
Gifford & Partners 46
Glamis Castle 75
Gefton, Bill 123
Gormley, Antony 85
Gracie, Vernon 15
Grainger Market 41
Grainger, Thomas 41
Grainger Town 42
Greathead, Henry 114
Green, Benjamin 117

Green, John and Benjamin 24
Grenville family 29

HRH the Duke of Edinburgh 17
HRH Queen Elizabeth the Queen Mother 35
Hadrian, Emperor 46
Hamilton, David 40
Hawks, Sir Robert Shafto 31
Healy, Brendan 21
Hepple, Wilson 32
Holy Jesus Hospital 22
Howdon 47

Ingham, Robert 123

Jarrow 47
Jesmond 29
Johnstone, William 118

Keelmen's Hospital 22–3
Kemp, W.B. 92
Kenton Colliery 48
Kilburn White Horse 118
Killingworth 44

Law's Herbal Supplies 87
Lemington glass cone 45
Liddell, Thomas Henry 88
Lorraine 45
Lukin, Lionel 114

Manic Rabbit 39
Marks & Spencer Penny Bazaar 41
Marsden Grotto 124–5
Marsden White Horse 118–19
Marshall, Richard 34
Mazzini, Joseph 72
Millennium Bridge 46, 55
Mowbray family 108
Muñoz, Juan 121–2
Museum, John George Joicey 22

National Projectile Factories 63
Newcastle City Council 21
    Corporation 27
    Curling Club 82
    Freeman of 44
    North Shields Railway 15, 24
    Town Hall 17
    Town Moor 44
    United FC 42
North East Coast Exhibition 44, 92
Northern Rock Foundation 38

North Shields Custom Quay 110
    Dolly 110
    Fish Quay 102
Norvell, John 95

Ouseburn 15
    Farm 24
    School 43
    Viaduct 24

Paine, James 76
Parsons Polygon 40
Parsons, Sir Charles 40
Peel, Dolly 123
Pegram, Bertram 114
Pevsner, Nikolaus 17
Phillips Fine Art Auctioneers 98
Pilgrim Street 30
Pill Box, Preston 105
Prior's Howen, Tynemouth 109

Quayside Business Development Centre 43

Ravensworth Castle 88
Rich, Frank Wise 43
Richards, Christopher 77
Ridley, George 20–1
Rollo, Corporal Alexander 109
Ryton 80–3
Ryton Heritage Group 82

St James' Park Stadium 42
St Mary's Chapel 29
St Mary's Well 30
Sage (Gateshead) 55
Saltwell Park 91–2
Scotswood 48
Scott, Sir Peter 34
Second World War 48
Shibden Dene 73
South Shields 114–16
    Conversation Piece 121–2
Sports Day 53
Stephenson, David 36
Summerhill 73
Surtees, Aubone 33
Surtees, Bessie 32

Tempest, Nicholas 72
Threshold 53–4
Tostig, Earl 108
Town Moor Act (1774) 44
Tyne Bridge 98

Tyne & Wear Passenger Transport
    Executive 40
Tynemouth Castle and Priory 108–9
    Command Centre 106
    House of Correction 103–4
    Lodge Hotel 103
    Master Mariners' Homes 111
Tyneside Cinema 38
Tyne & Wear Metro System 26

University of Newcastle 49

Vaux & Co. Ltd 125
Victoria Tunnel 48

Wailes, William 91–2
Wales, Wales & Rawson 35
Weardale Iron & Steel Company 25
Welch, J. & Co. 24
Whickham 62, 94
    King George's Field 86
Whitburn, Red Cottage 117
Wiebeking system 24
Wilkinson Eyre 46
Willington 26
Willington Gut 24
Windy Nook 52, 58–9
Winstone, Mike 53
Wouldhave, William 114, 116